The Artwork of Kai Presedo

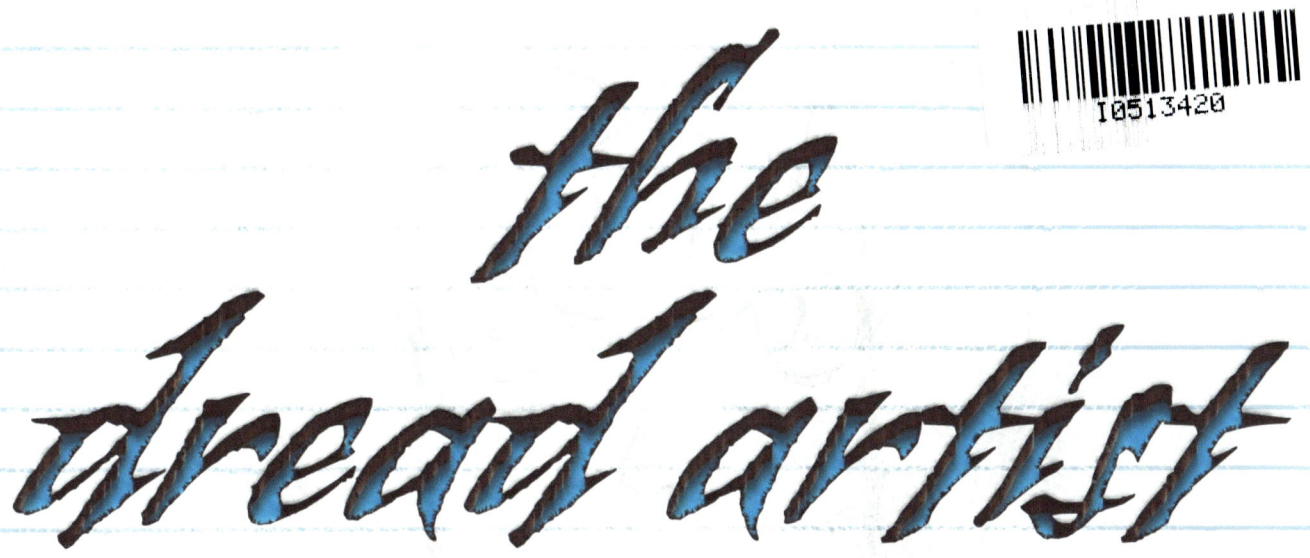

© 2019 by Kai Presedo
TM & Text copyright 2019 by Kai Presedo
Illustrations copyright 2019 by Kai Presedo

All rights reserved. Published in the United States by Dramenon Studios.
www.dramenon.com
www.presedo.net

The Artwork of Kai Presedo™ Volume 1 is © 2019 to Kai Presedo. The art and characters, incidents, and dialogue are products of the author's imagination and are not to be construed as real. Any resemblance to actual events or persons, living or dead, is entirely coincidental. None of the contents may be reprinted, except for purposes of review, without the written permission of Dramenon Studios. www.dramenon.com

We all start somewhere...

I am really passionate about drawing and hope to pursue it as a profession in the future.

My favorite subjects to draw are characters from the stories I have read or shows I have watched.

Kai

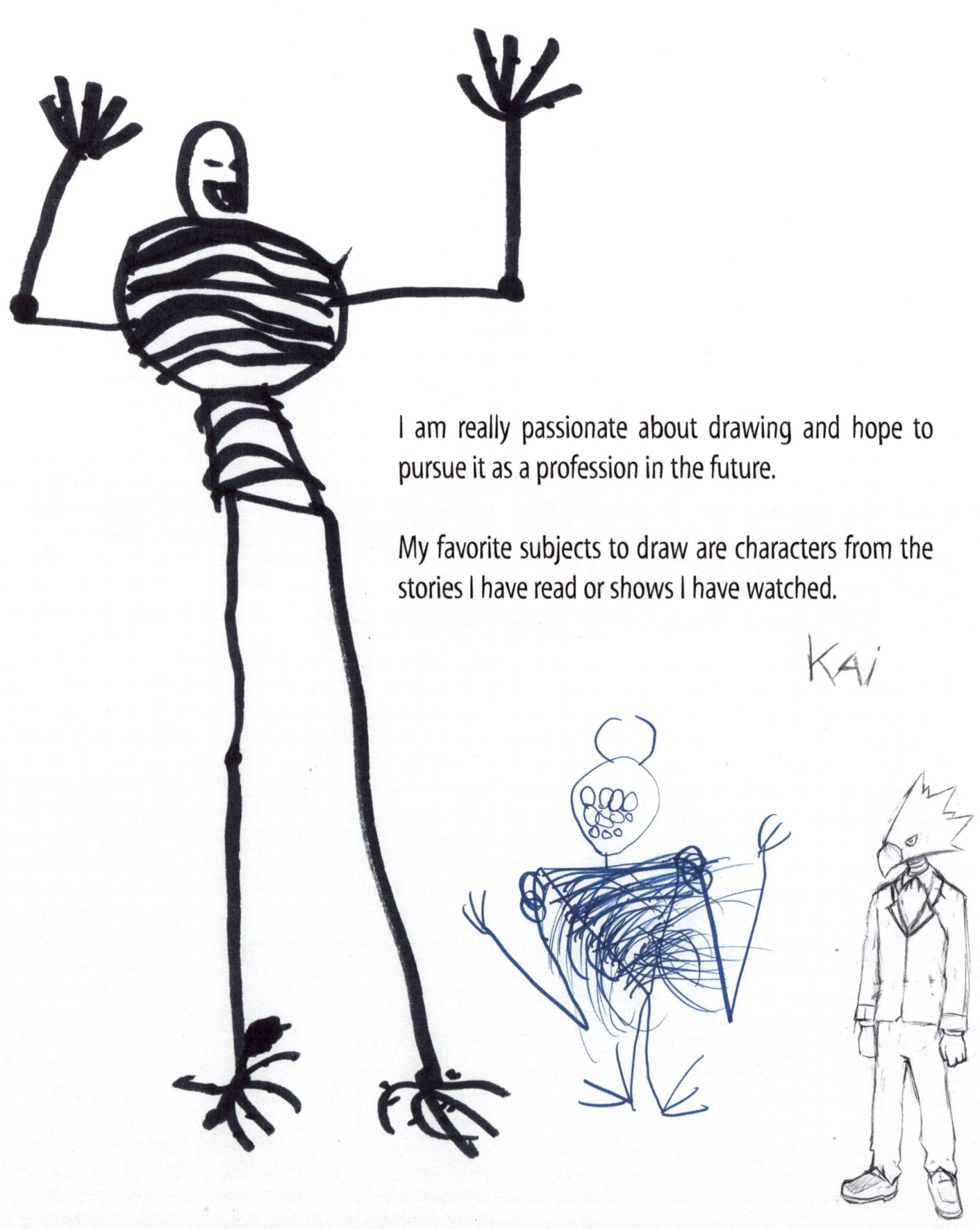

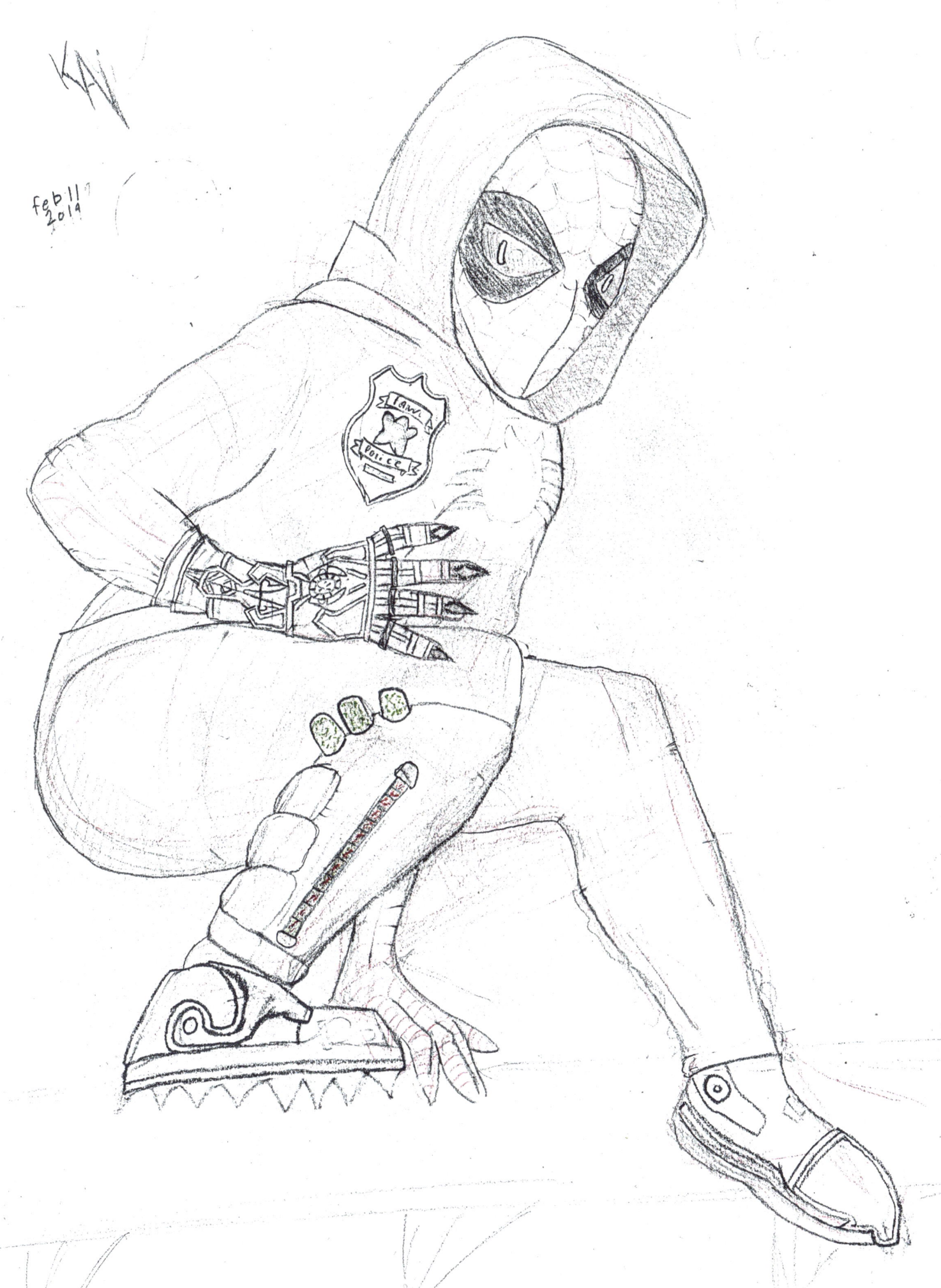

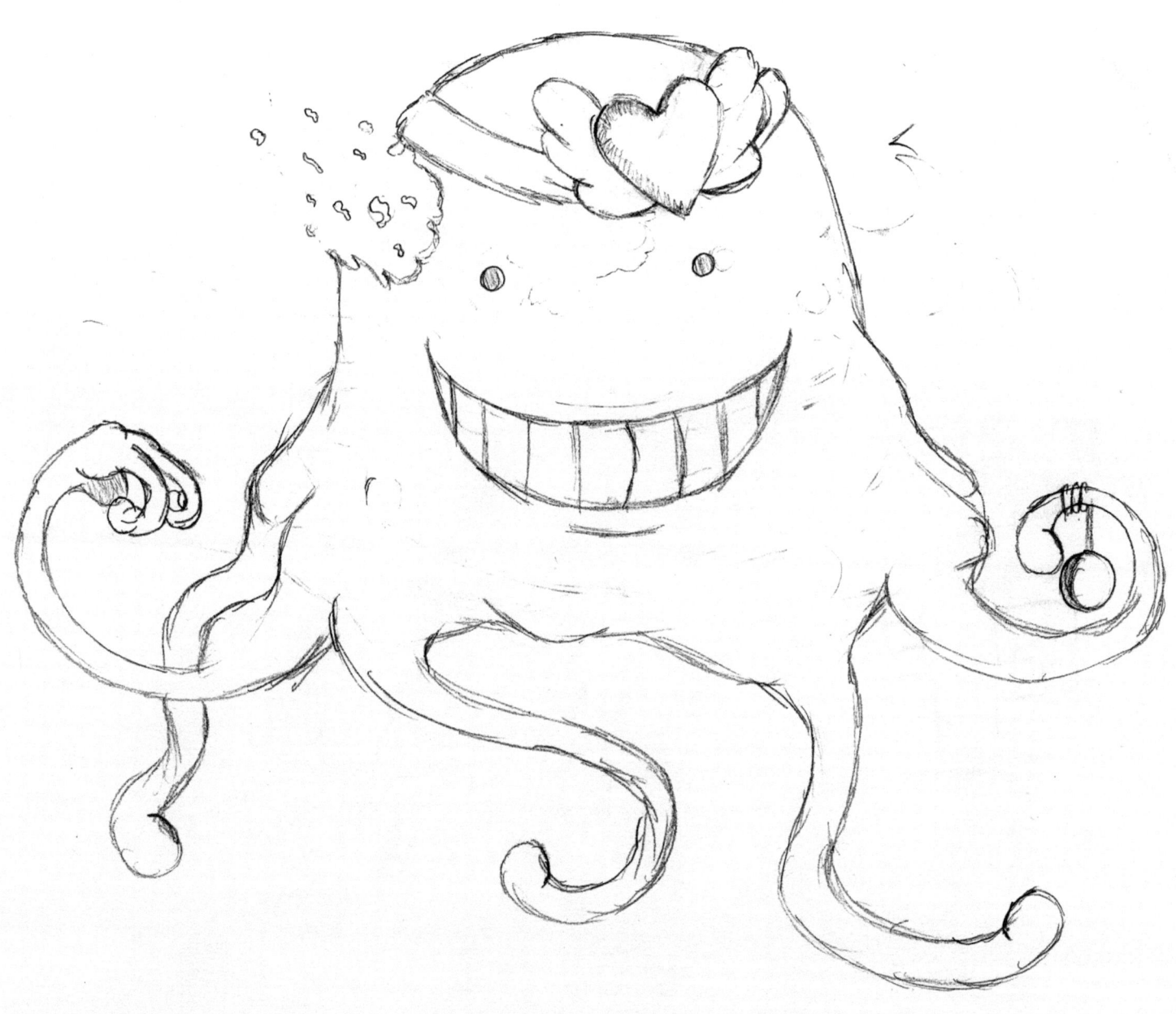

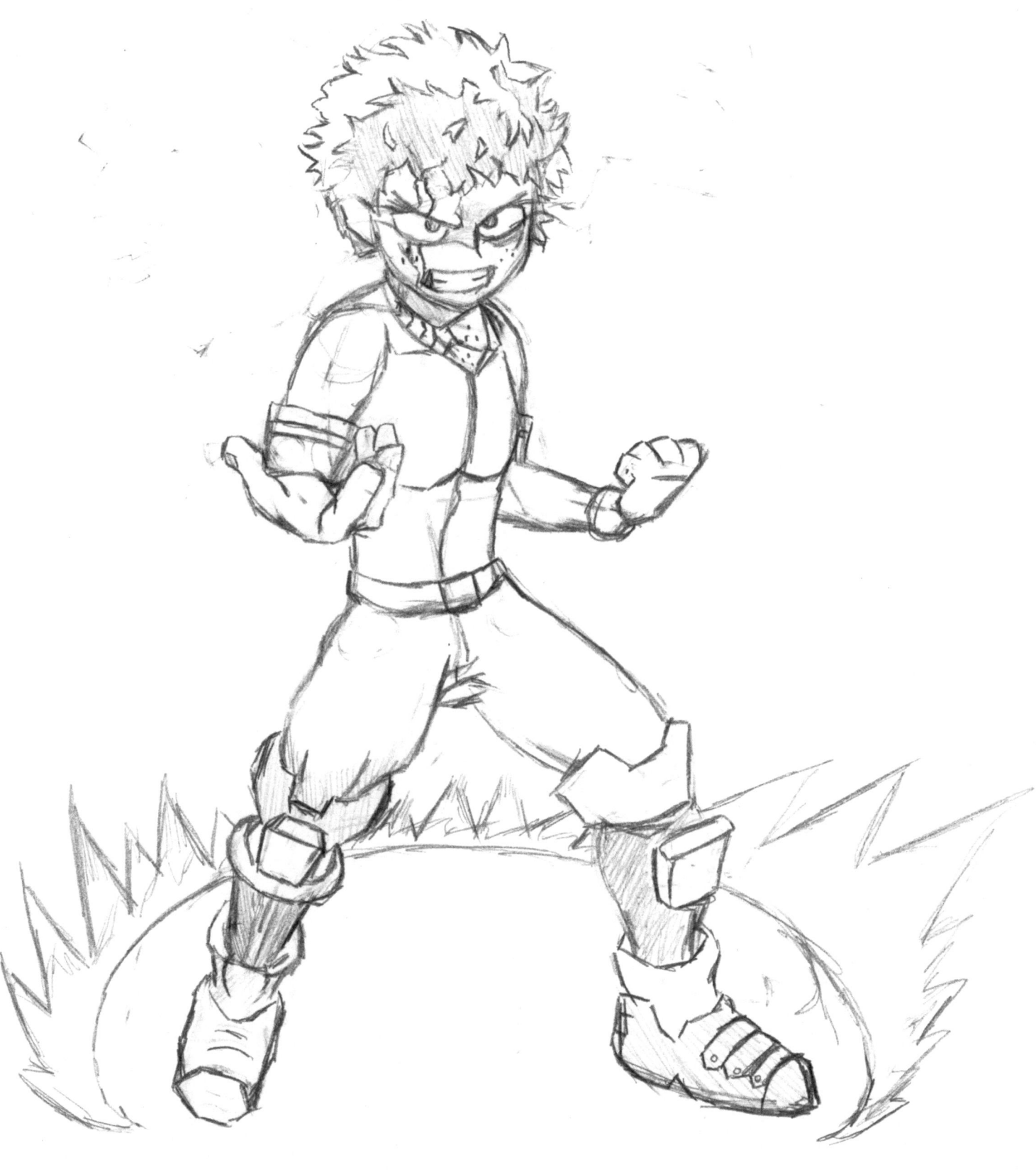

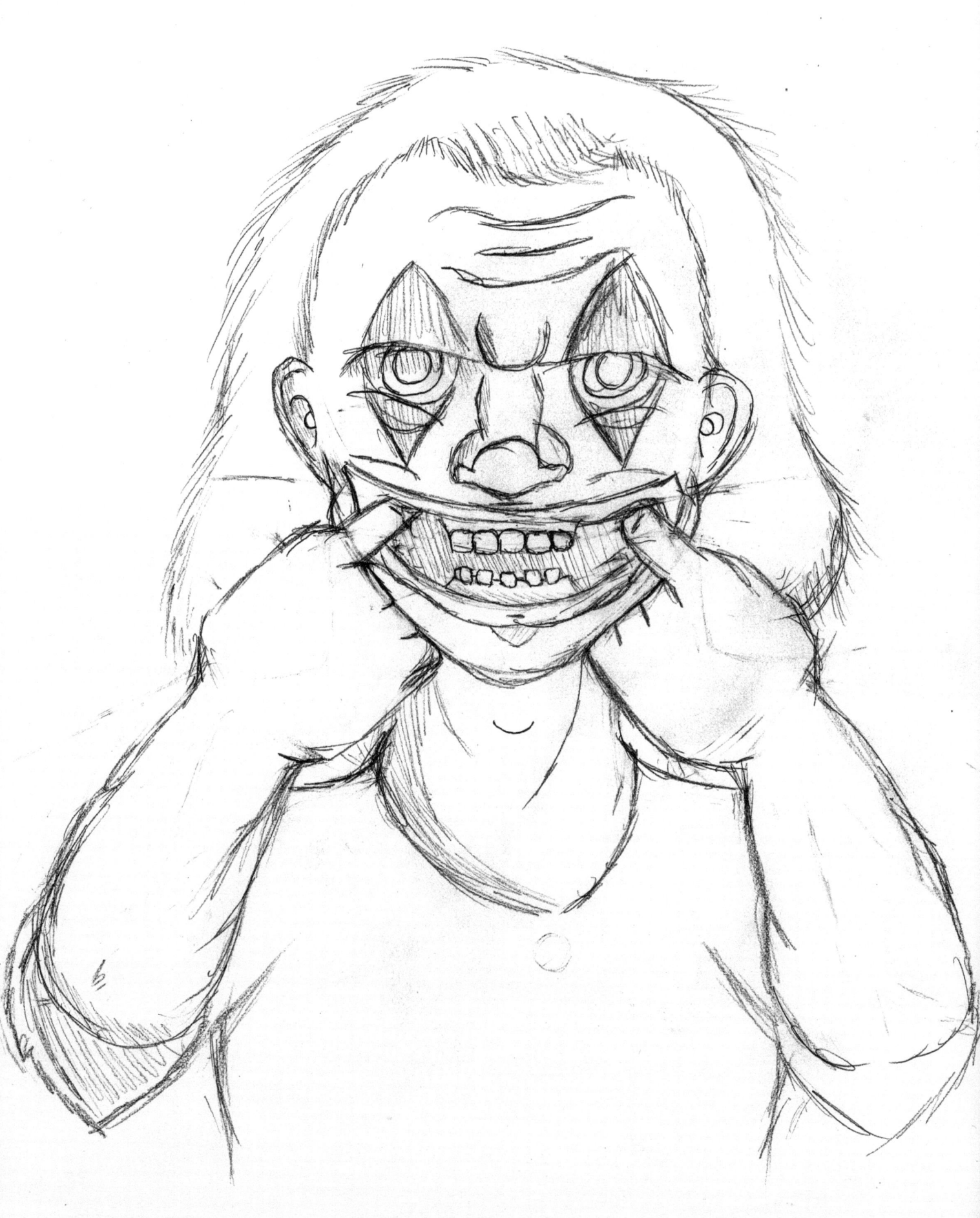

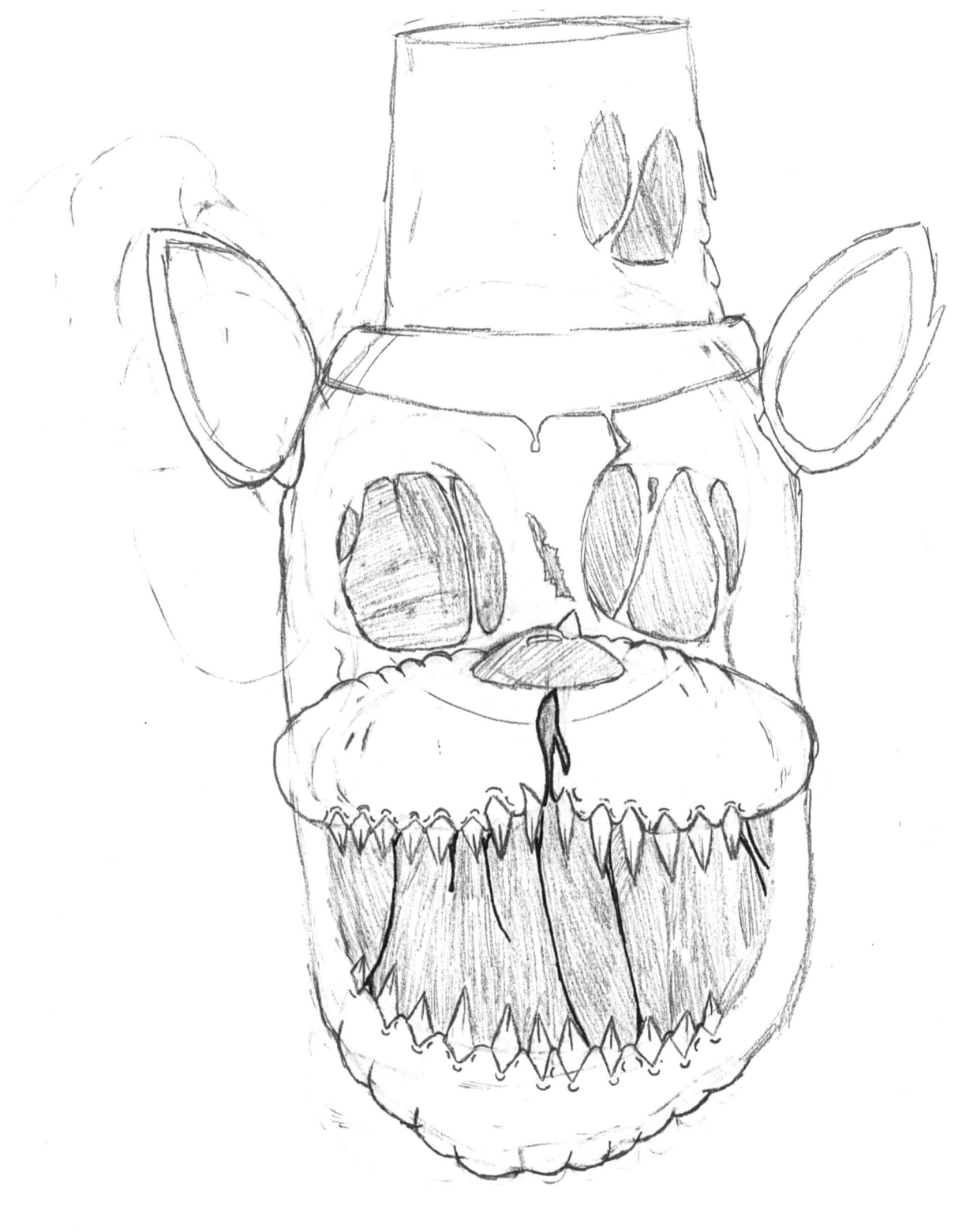

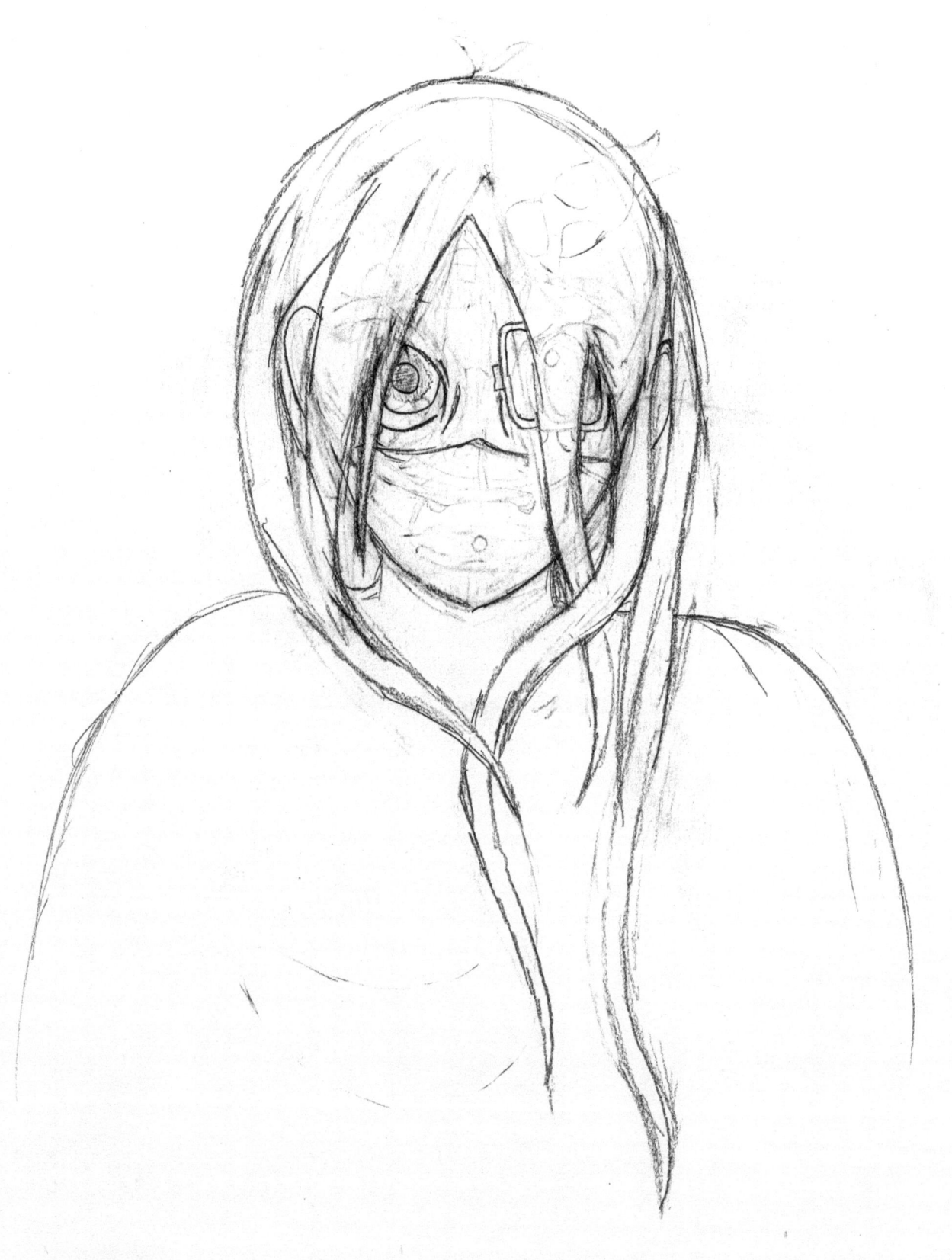

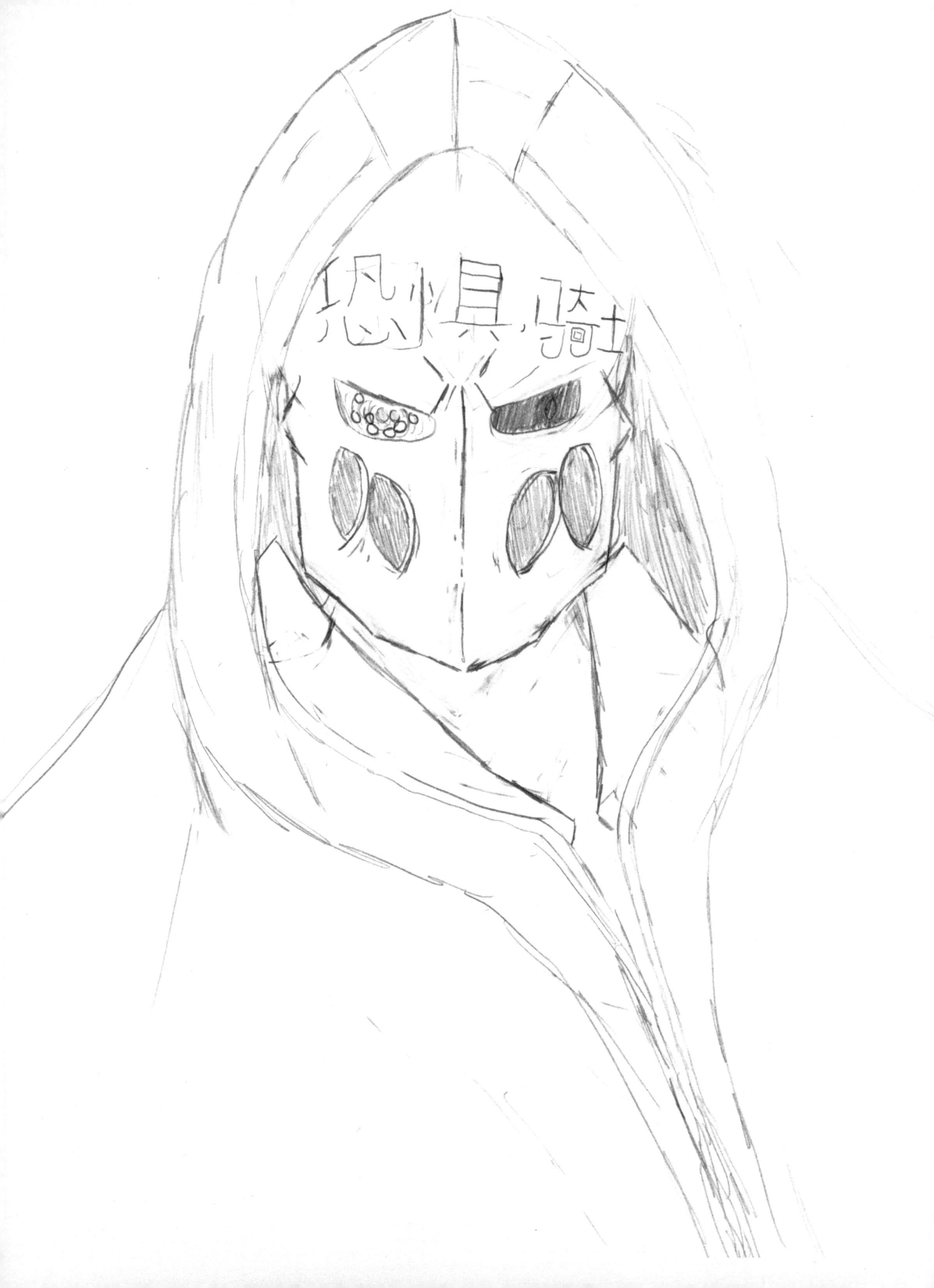

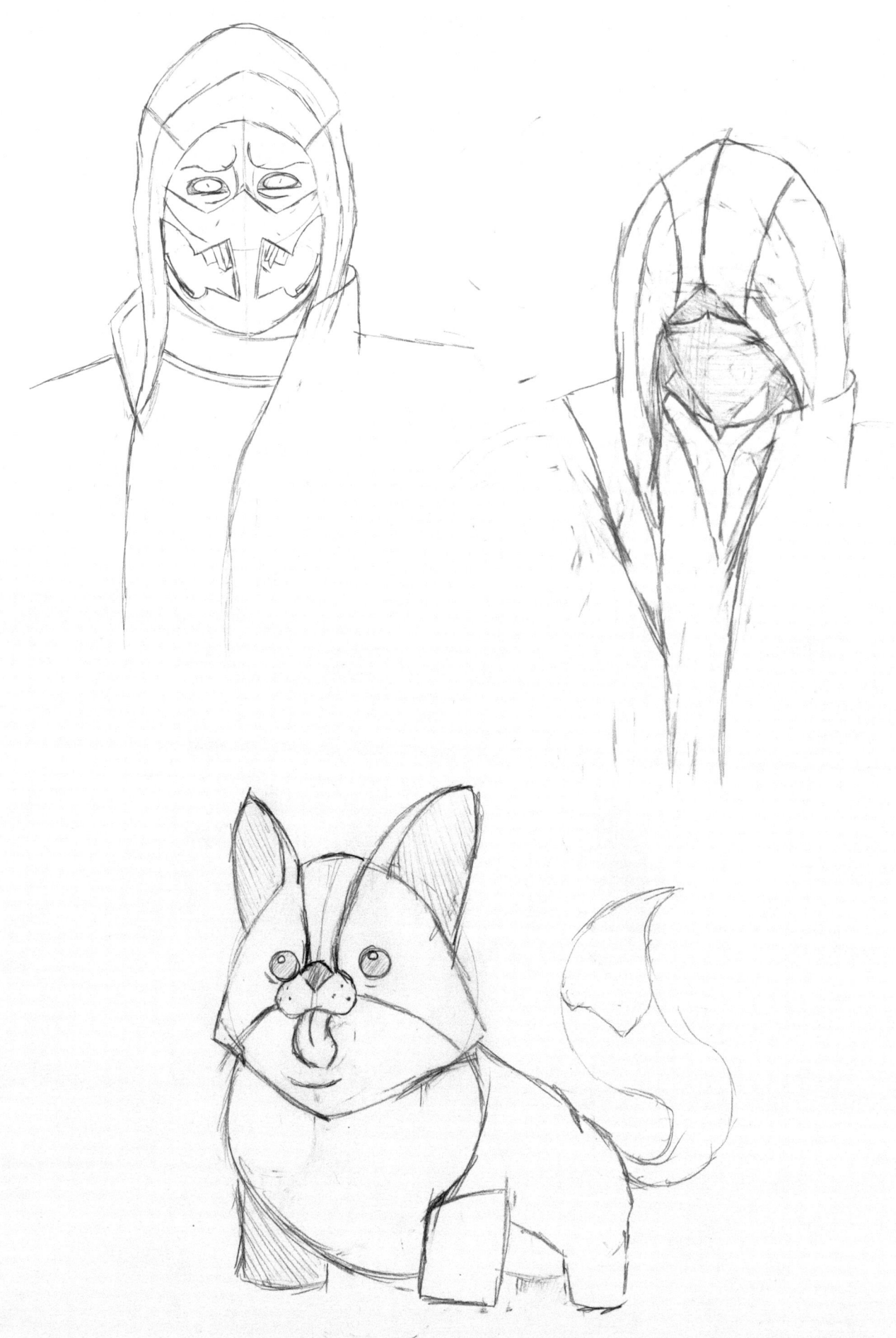

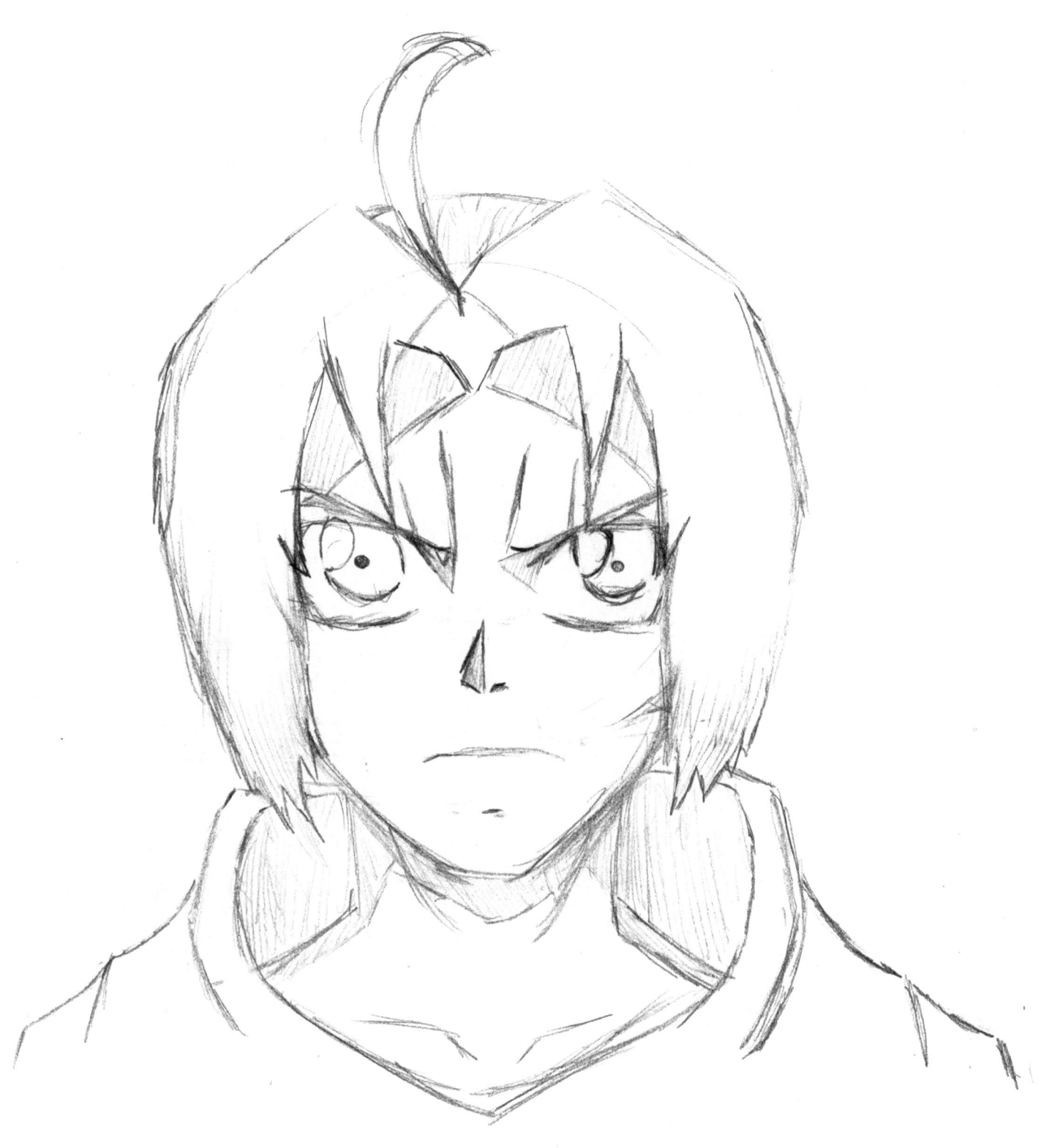

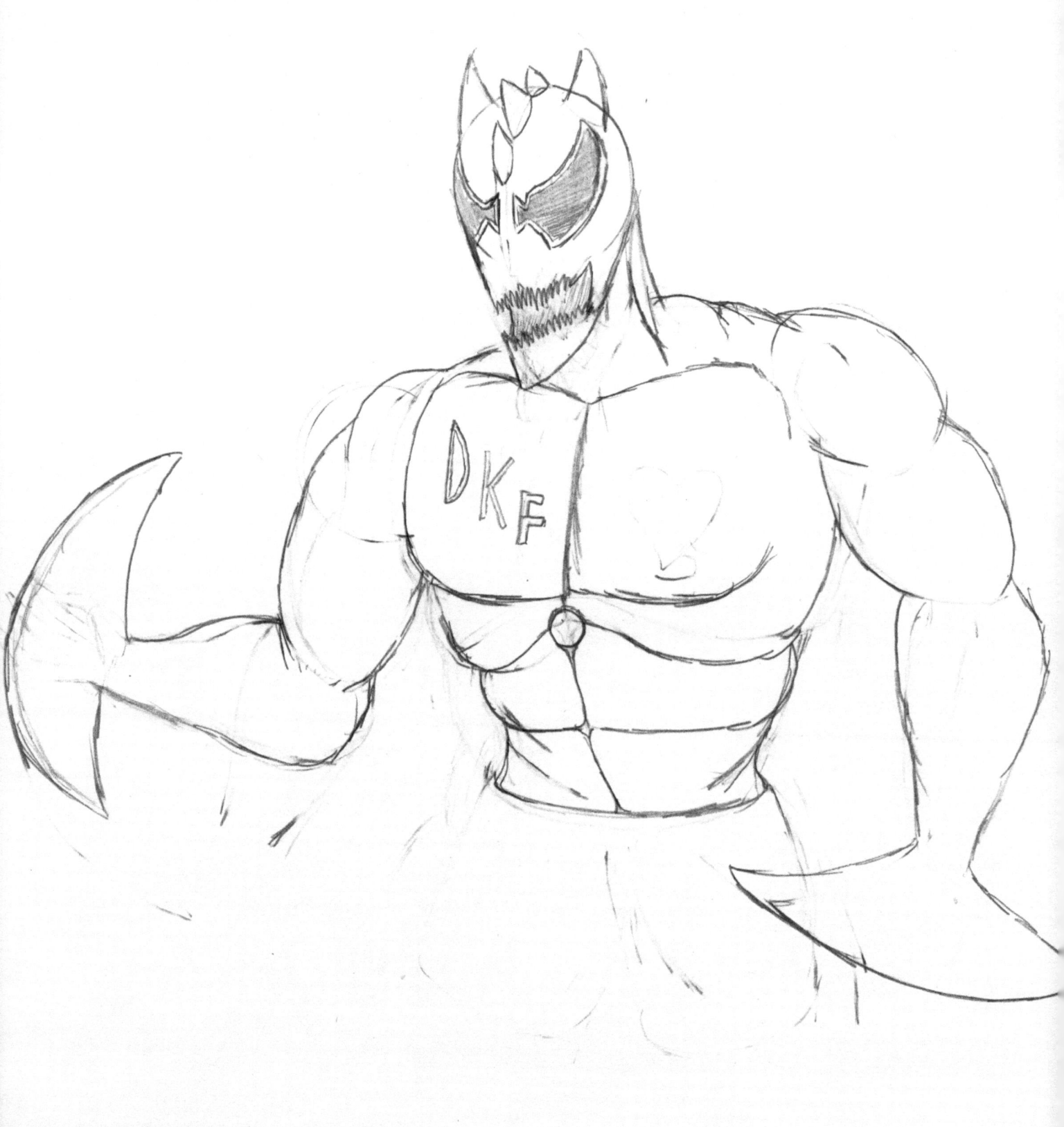

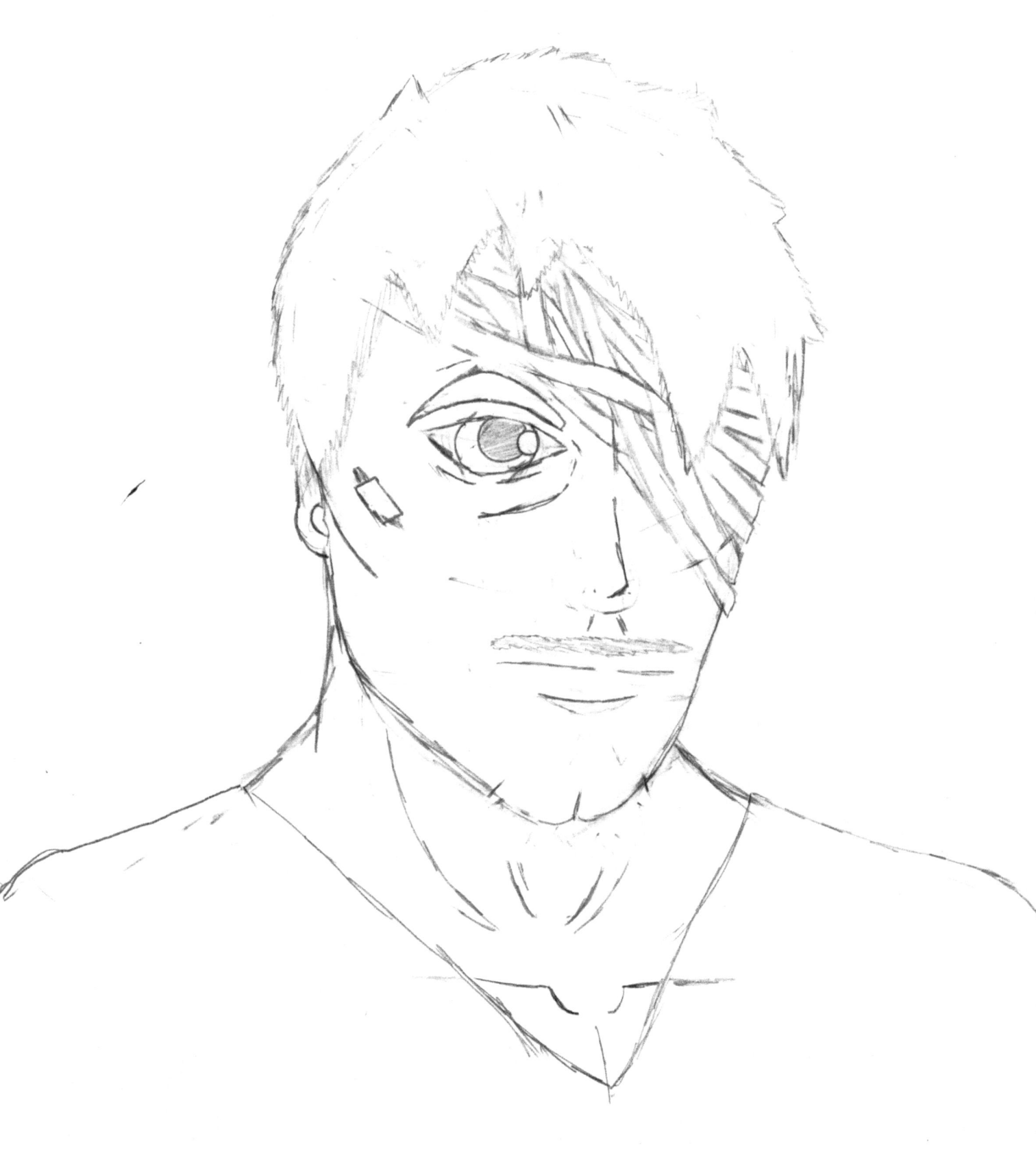

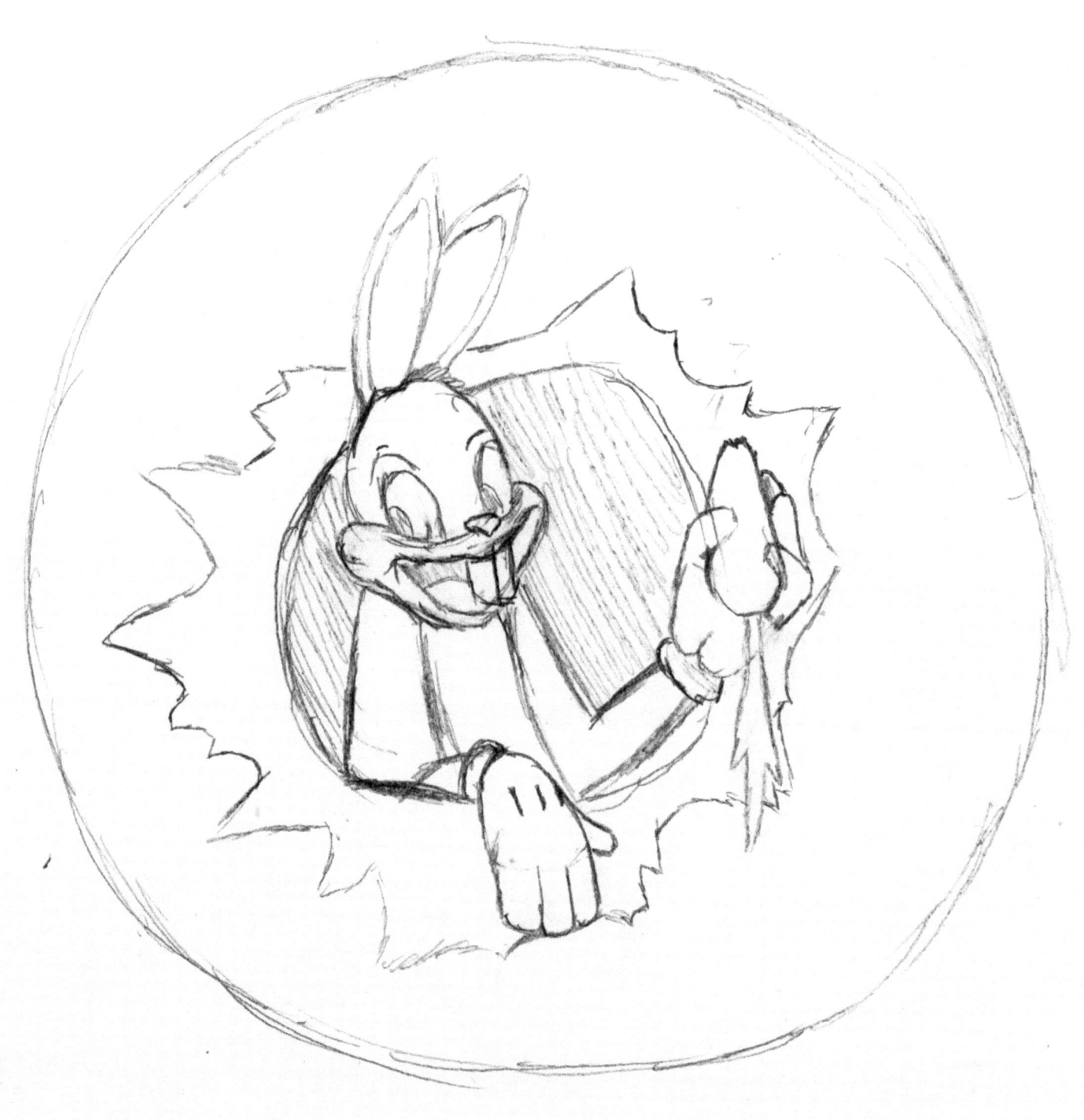

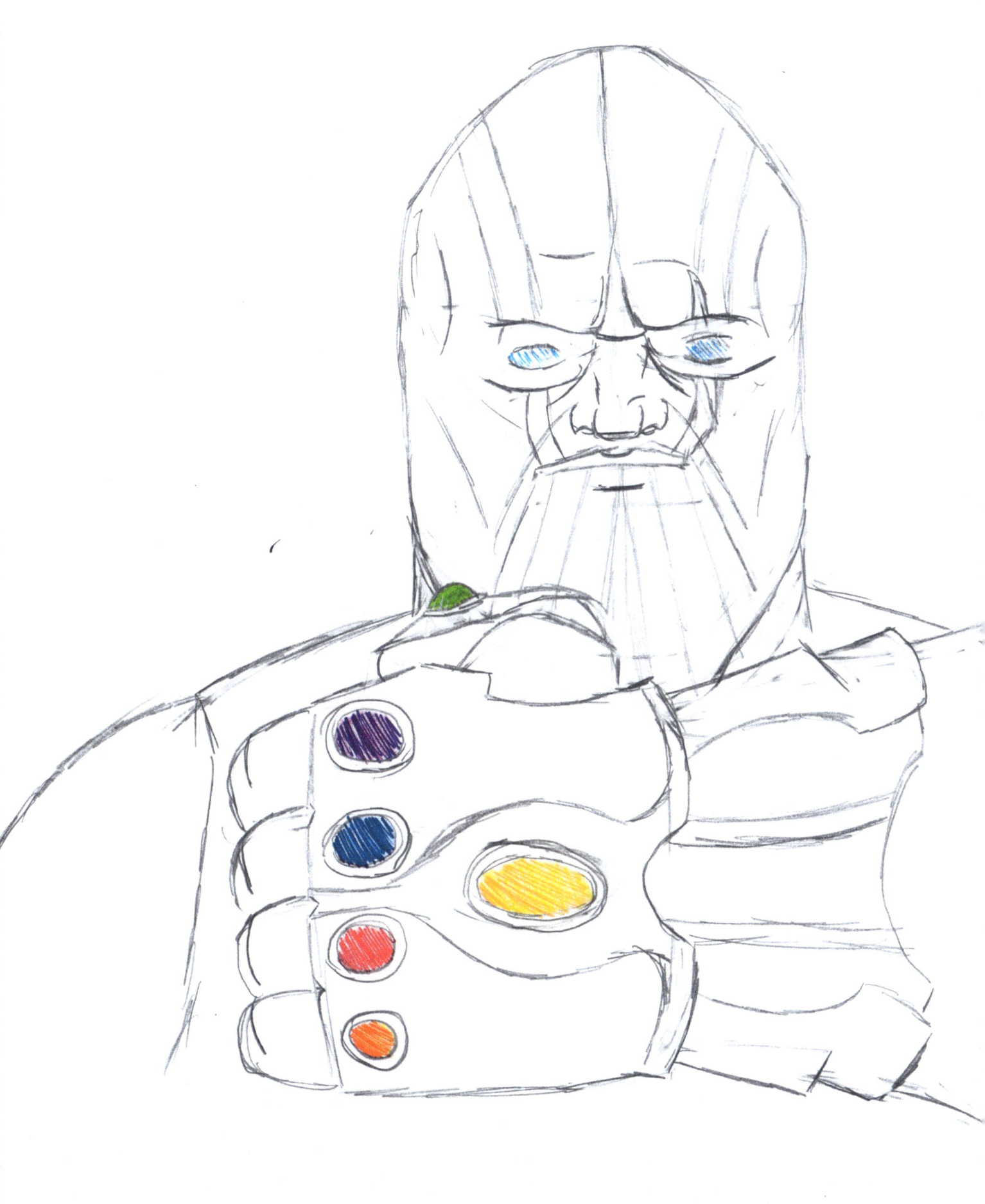

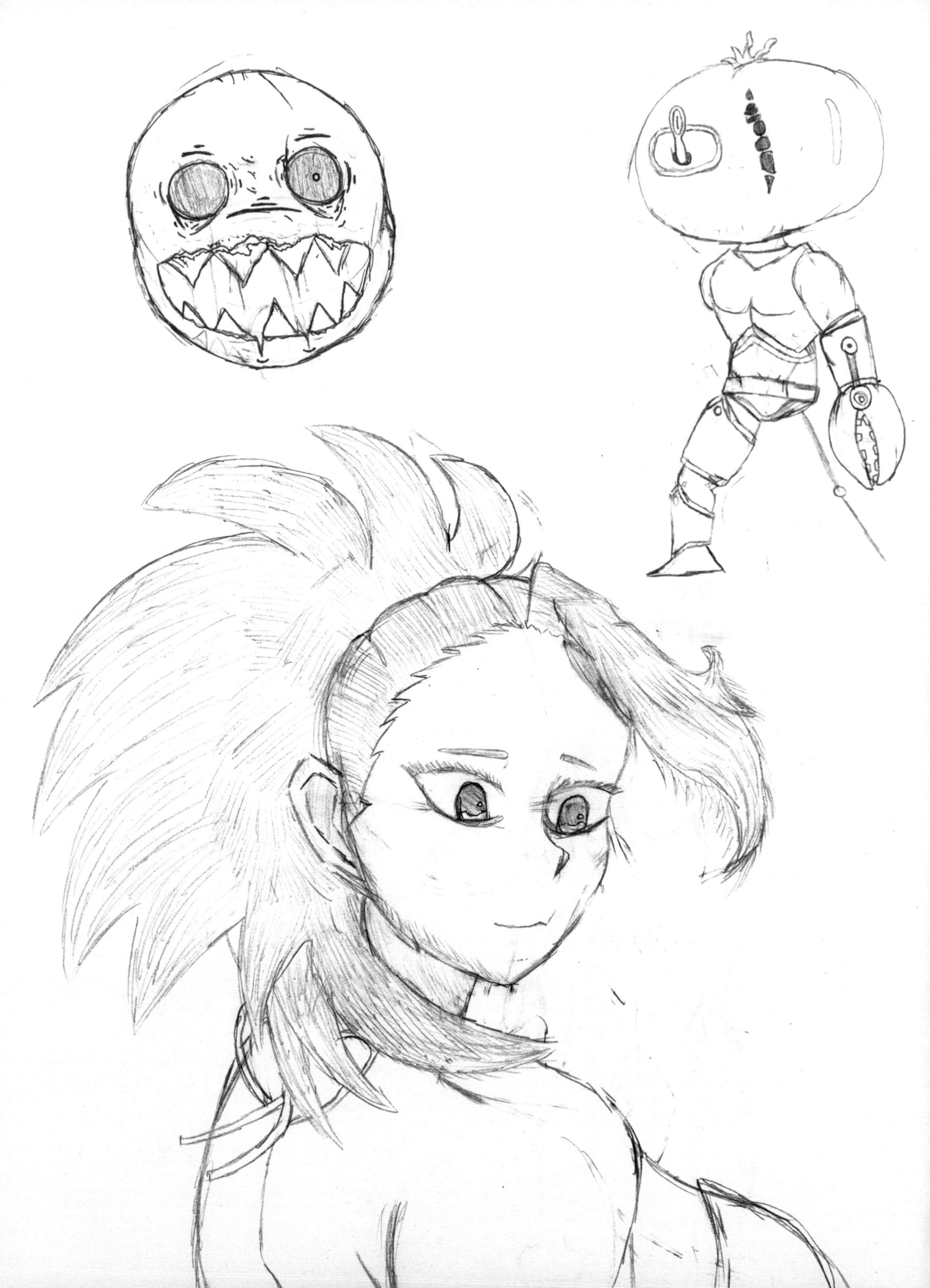

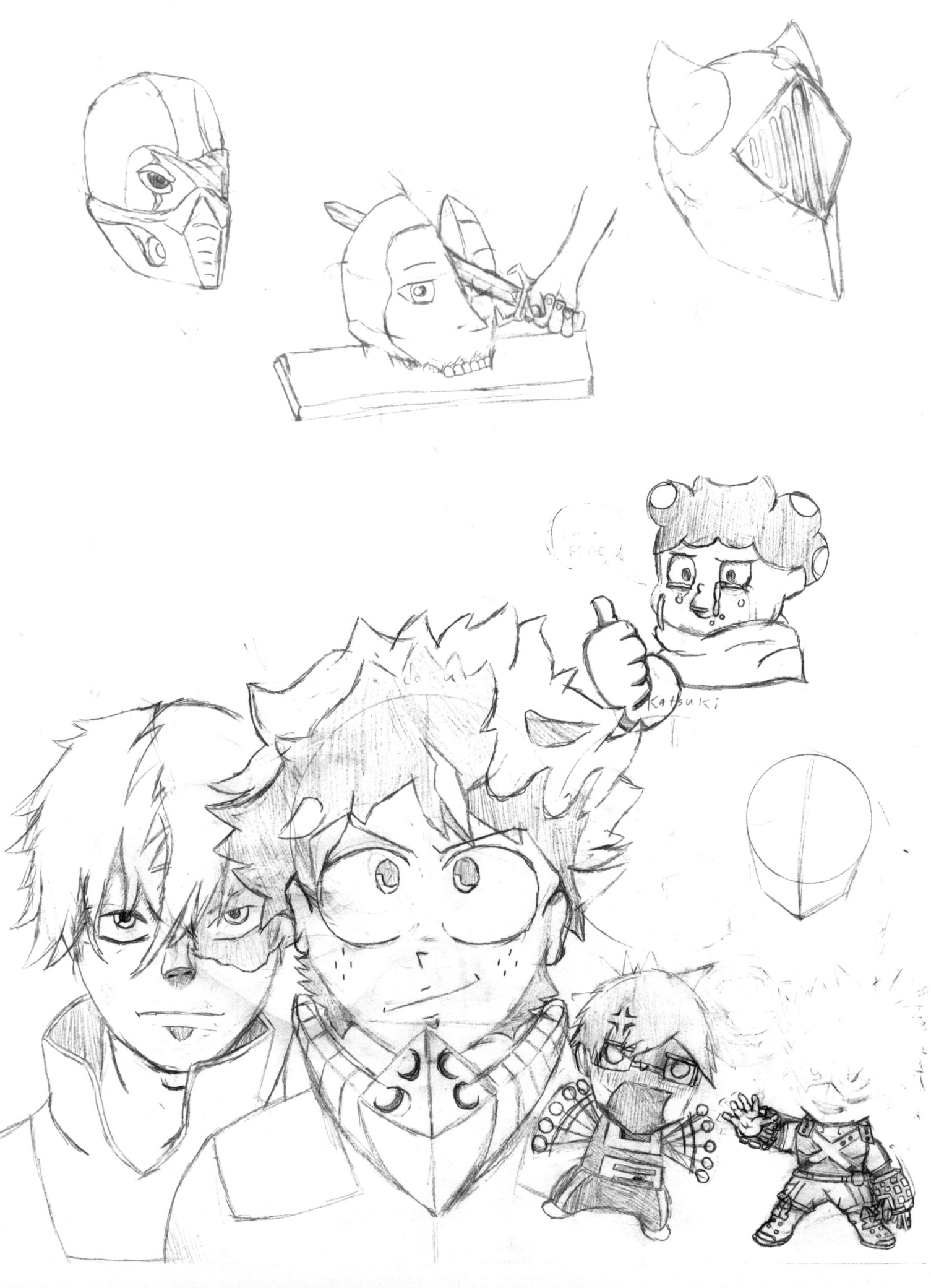

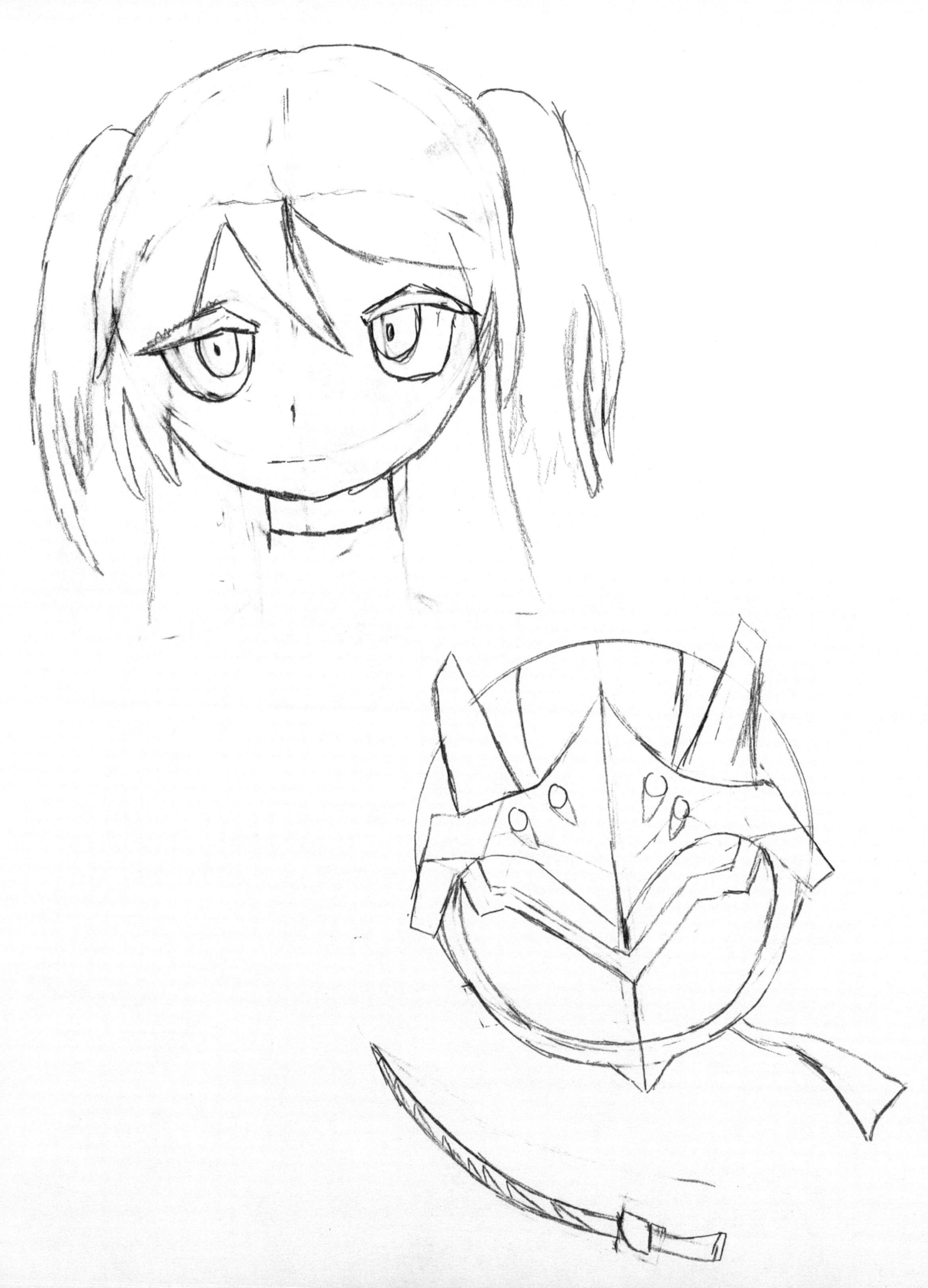

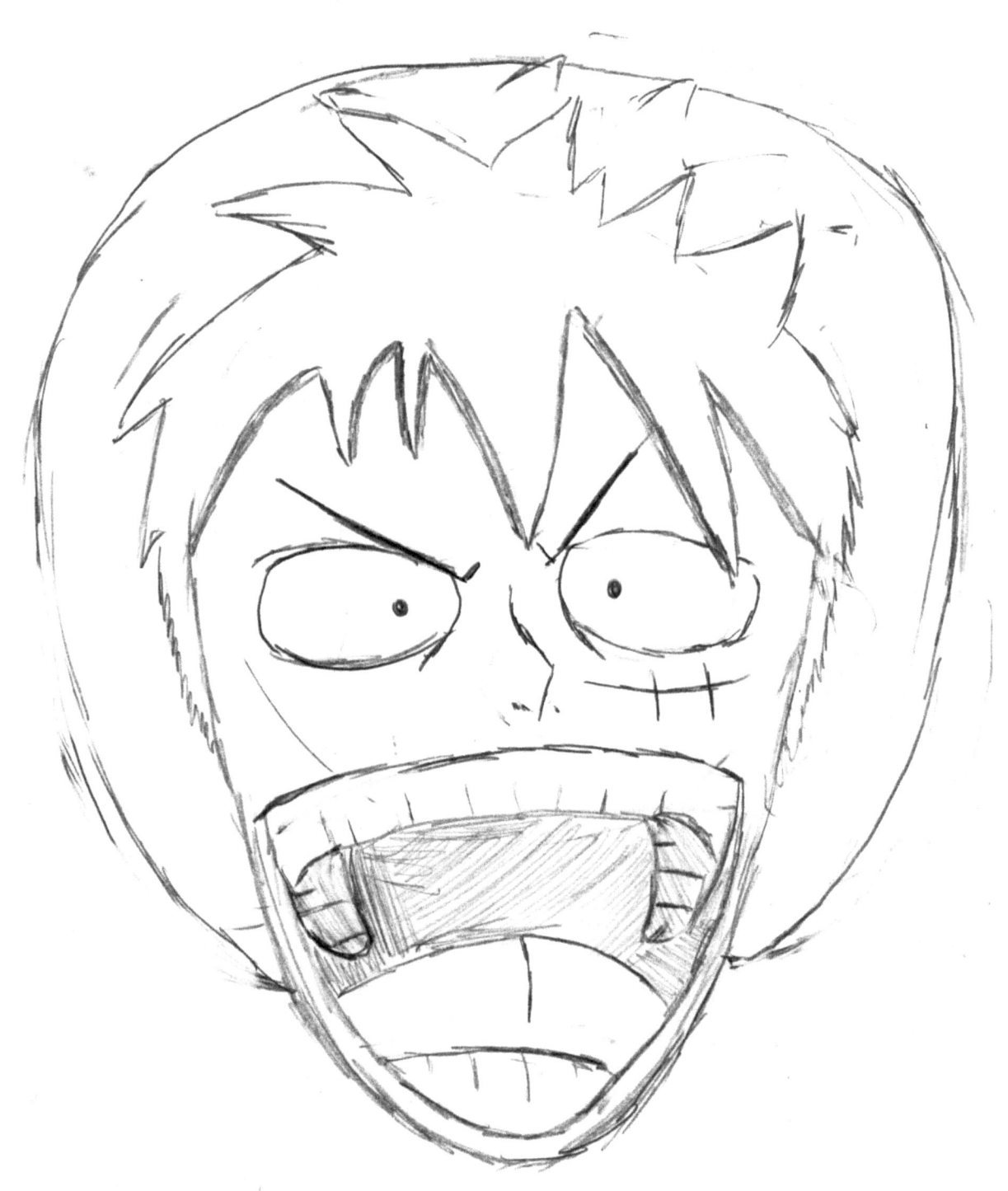

tokoyami

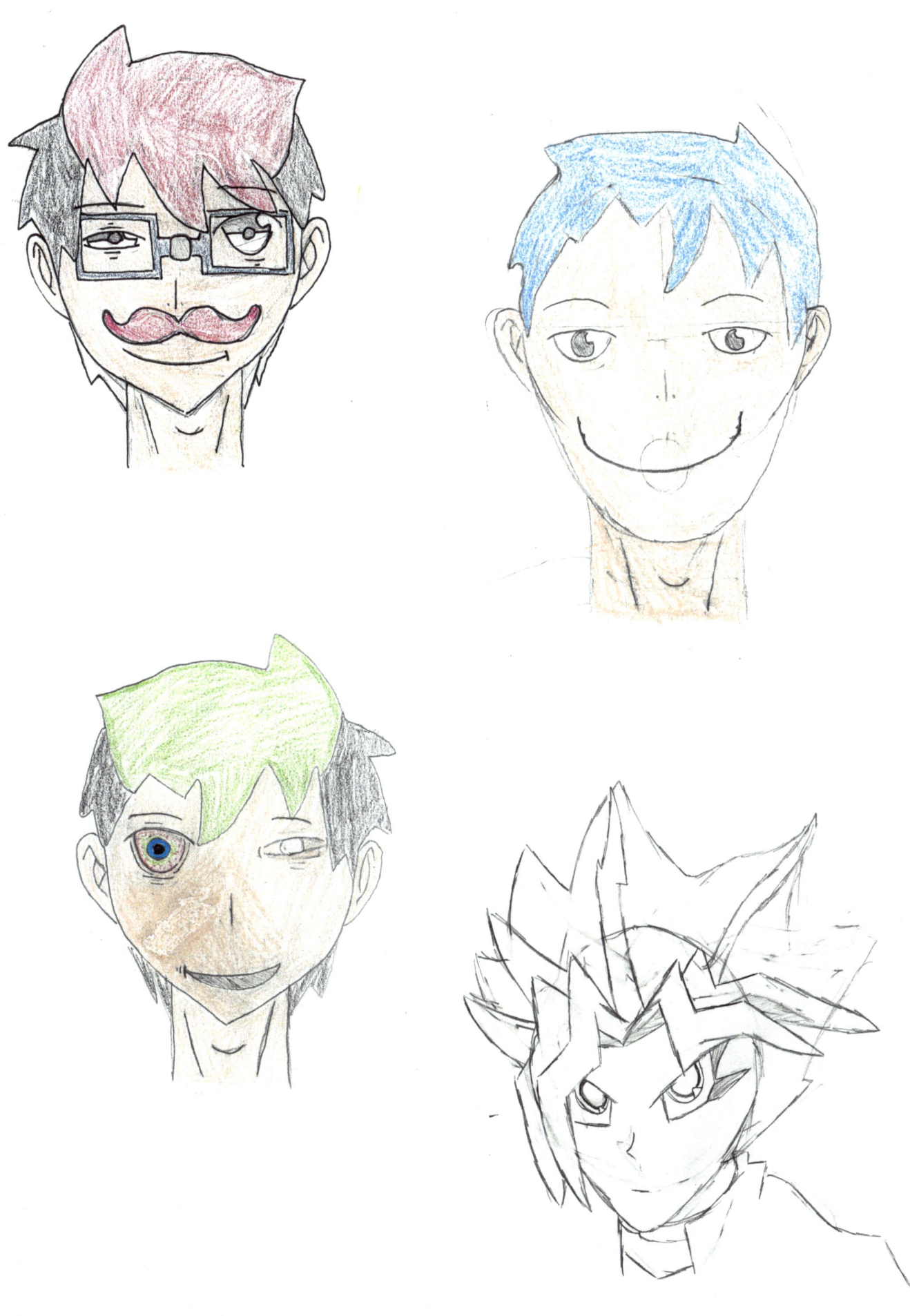

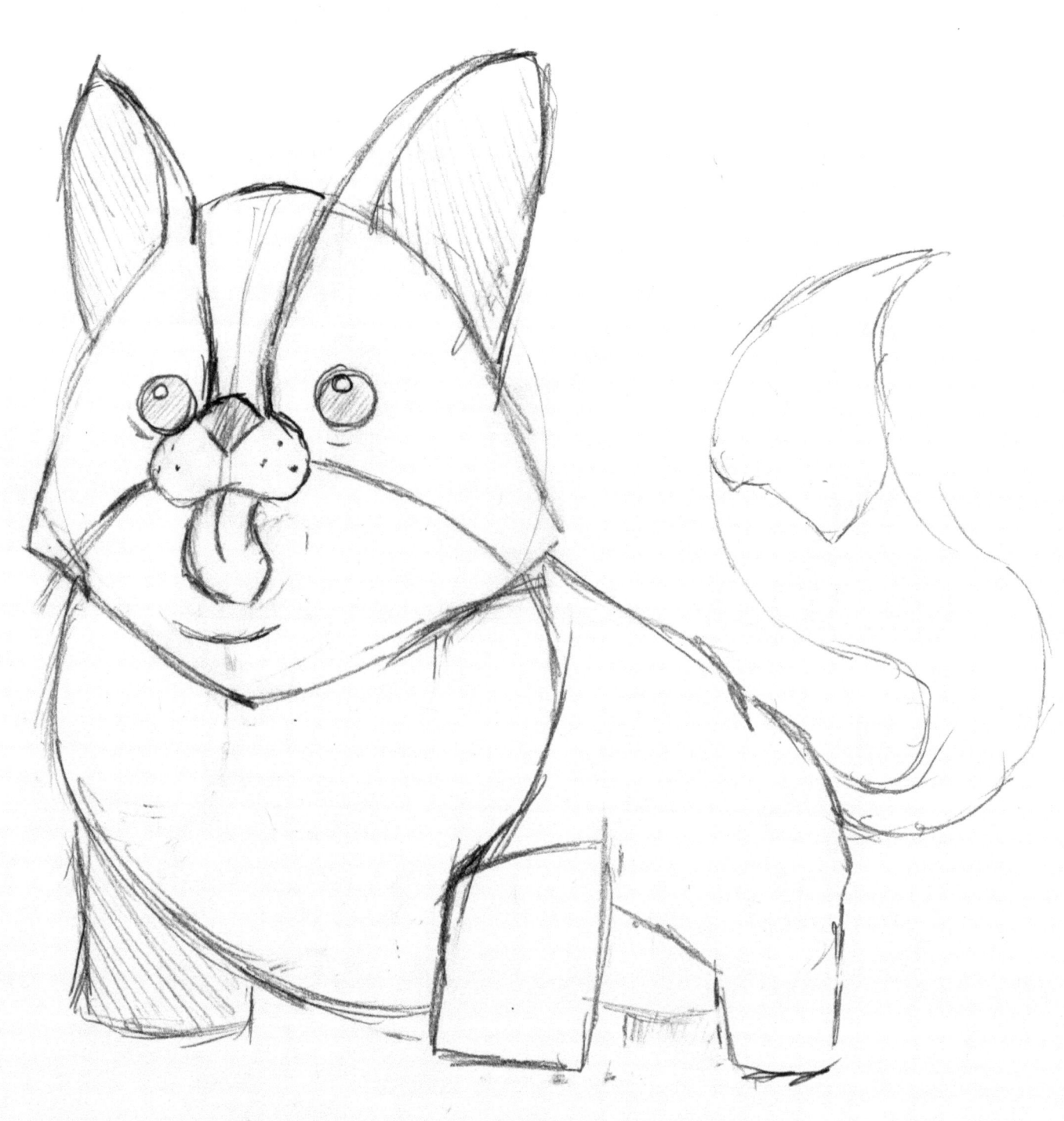

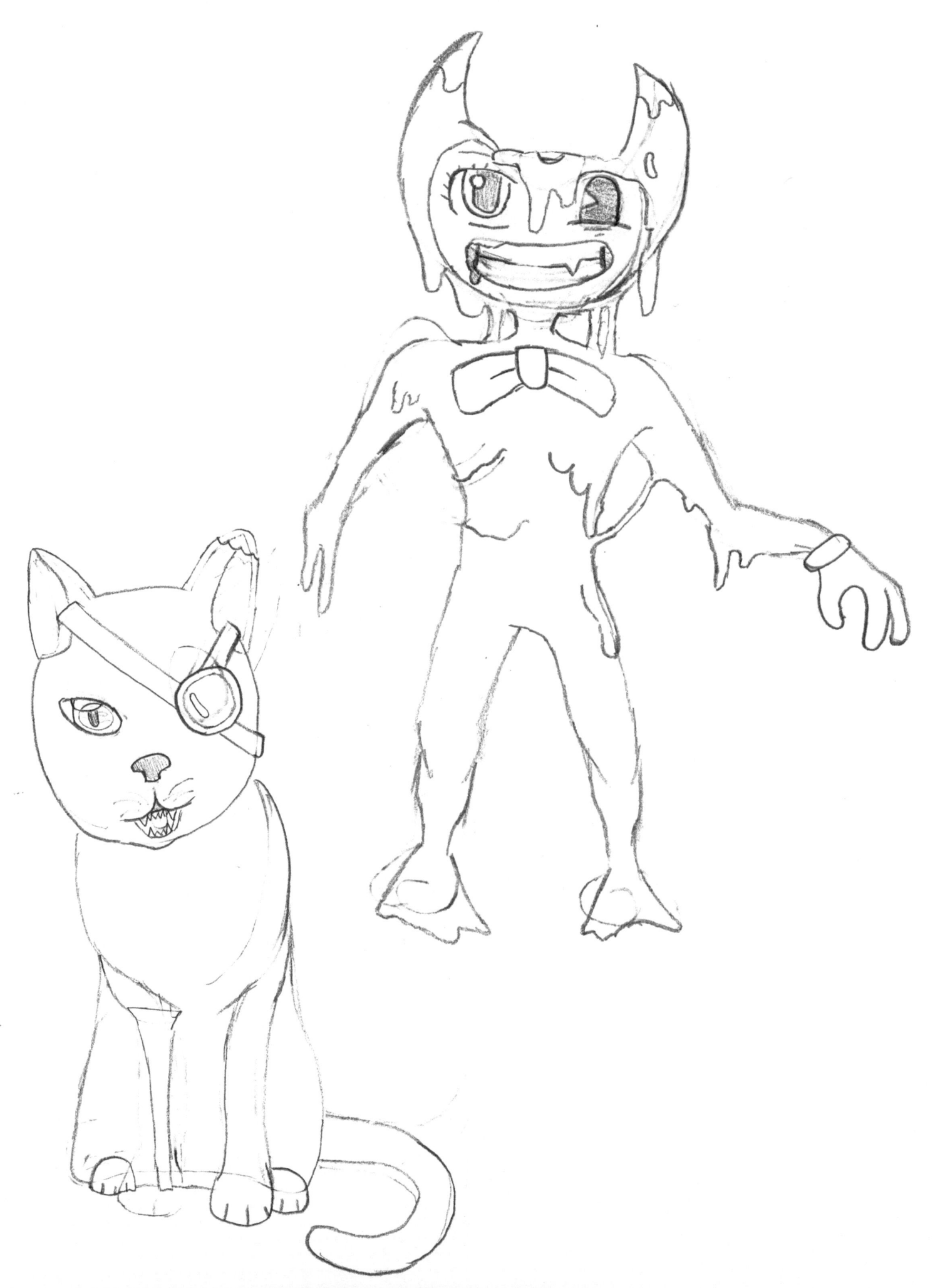

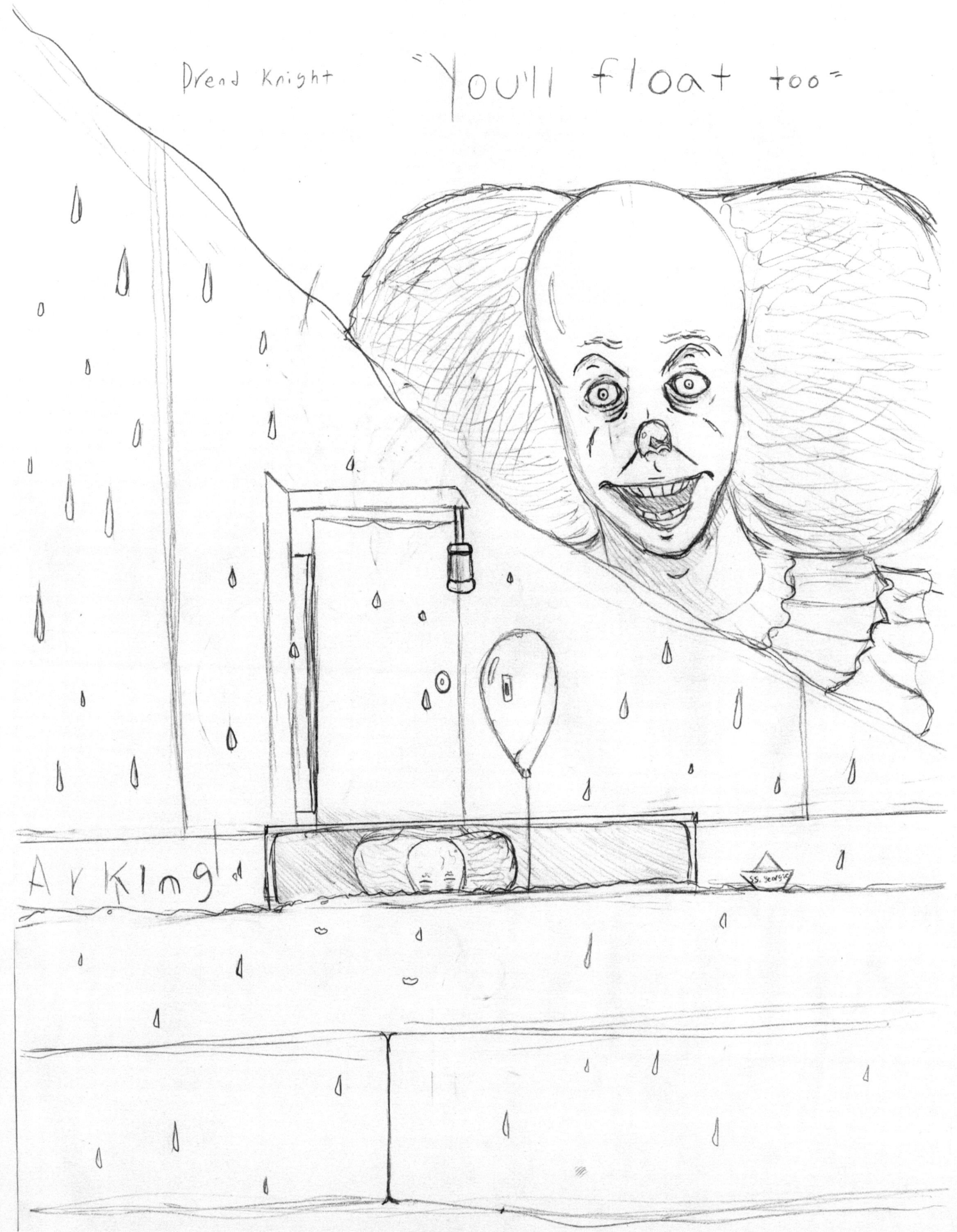

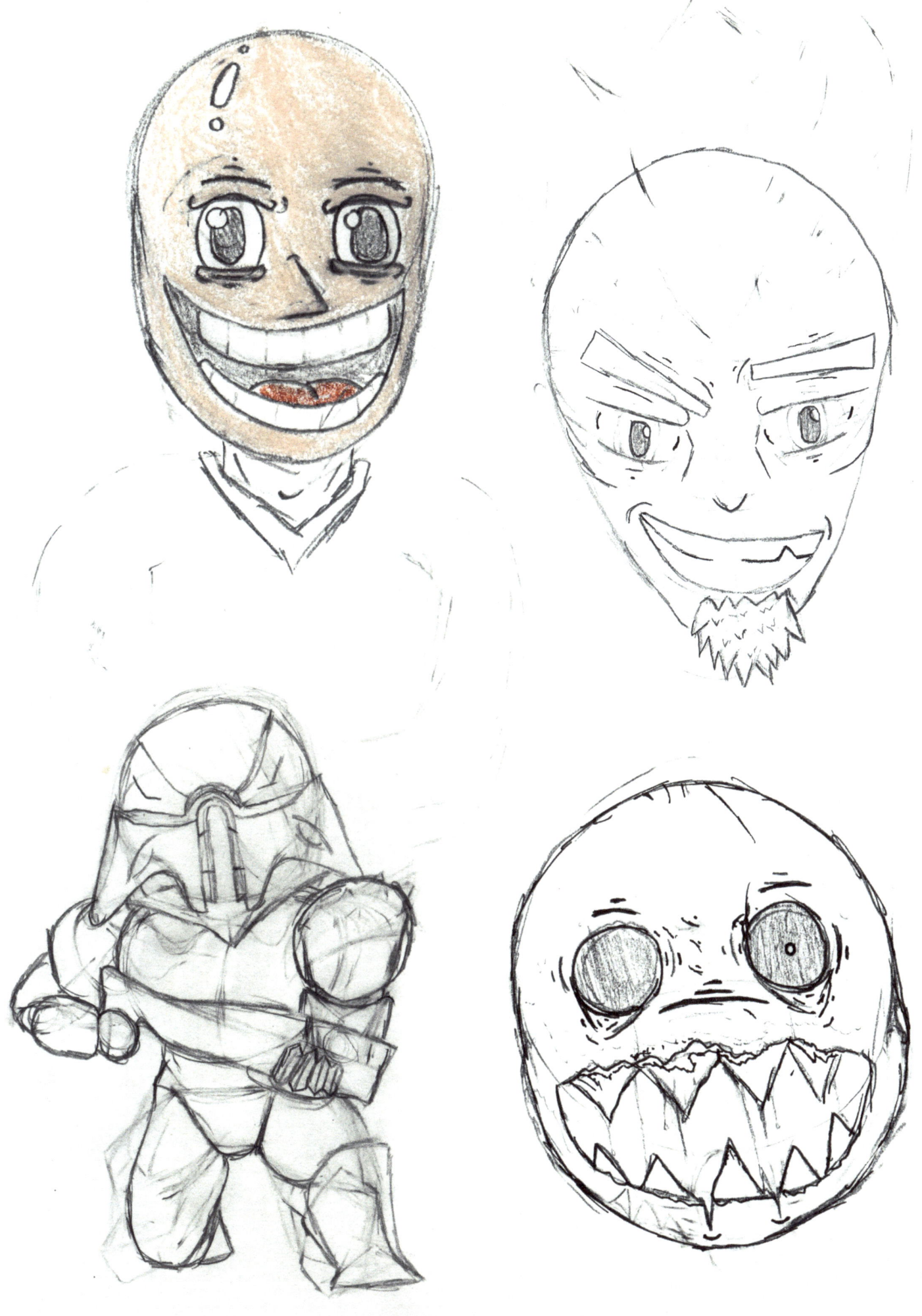

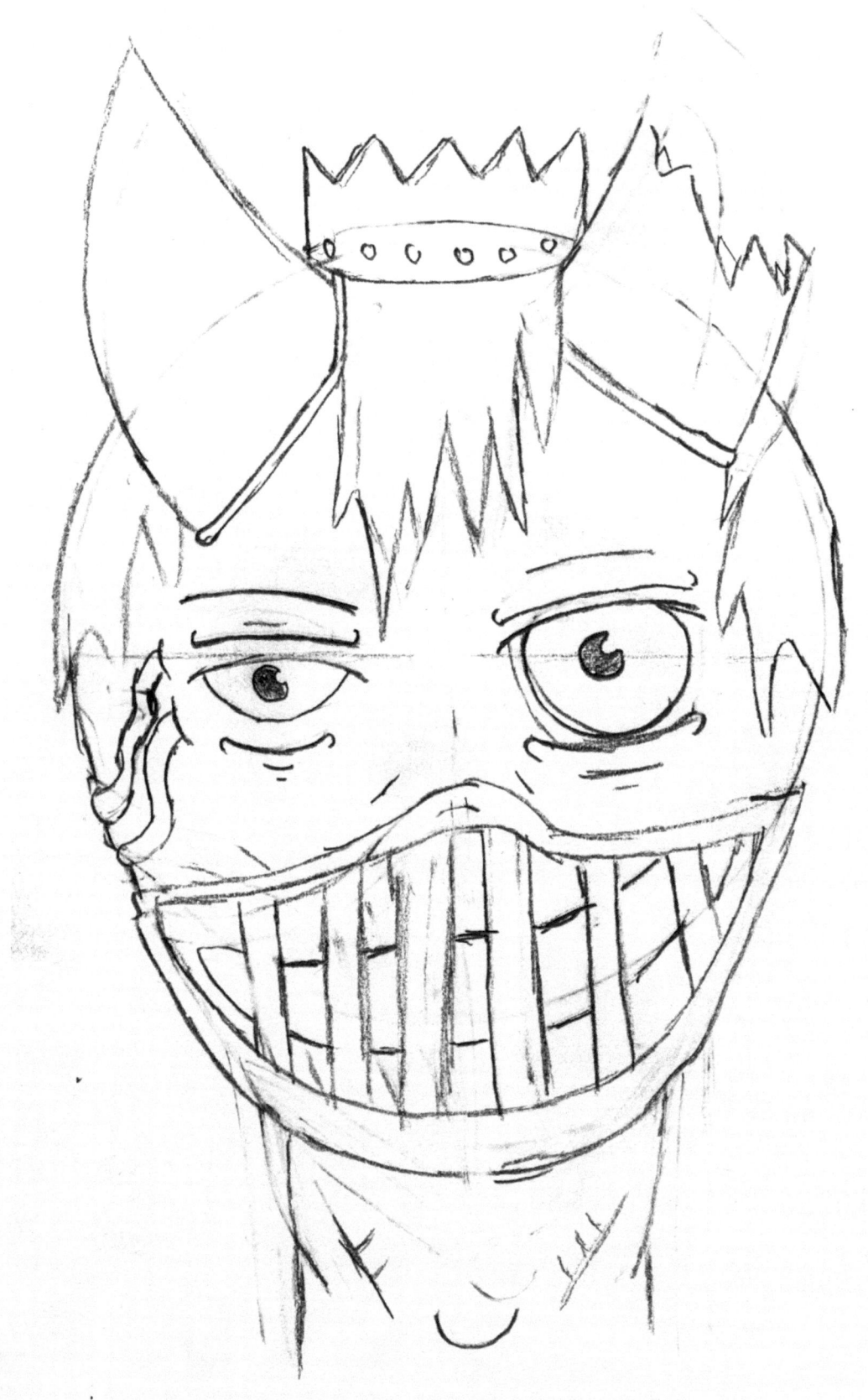

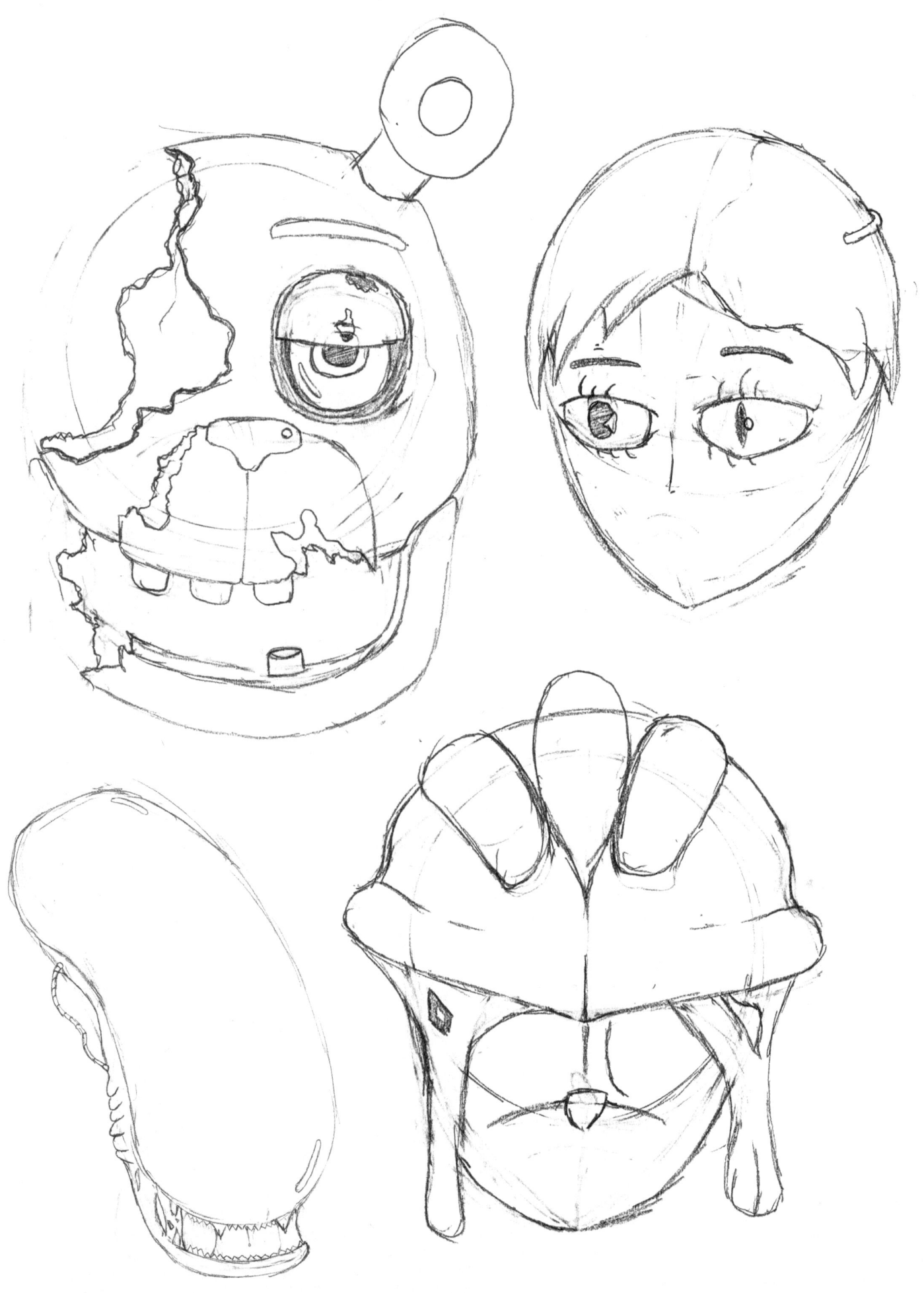

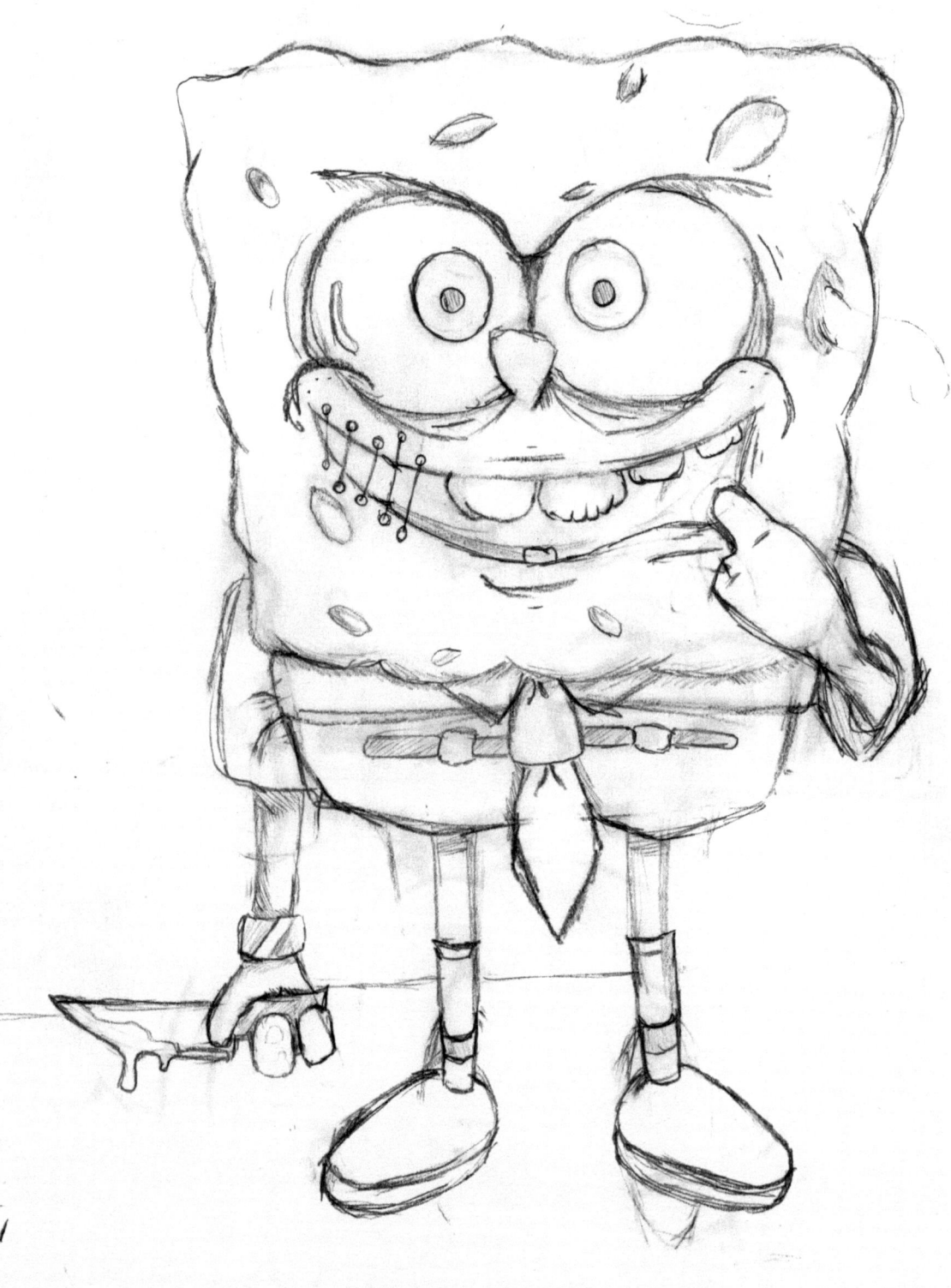

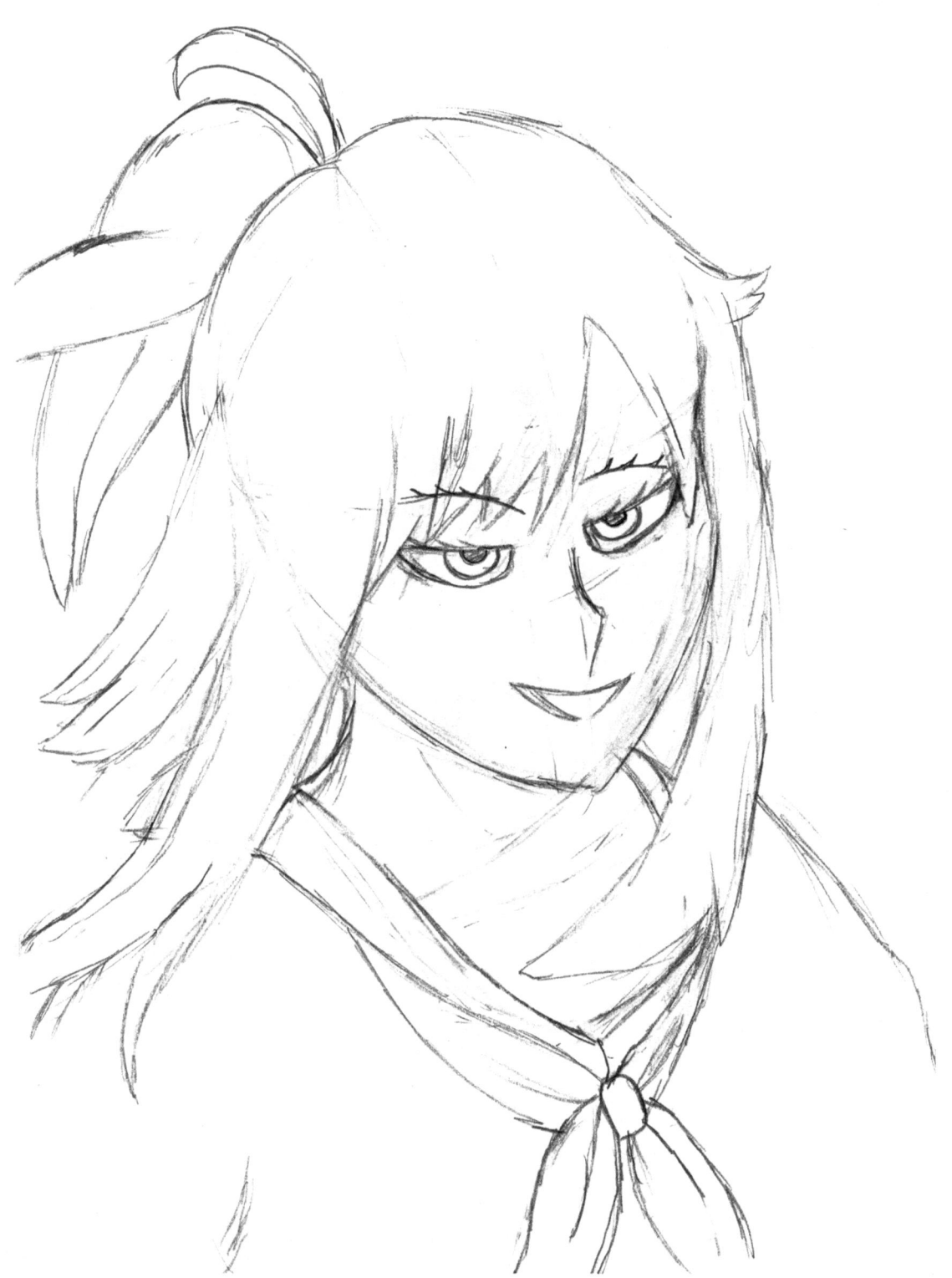

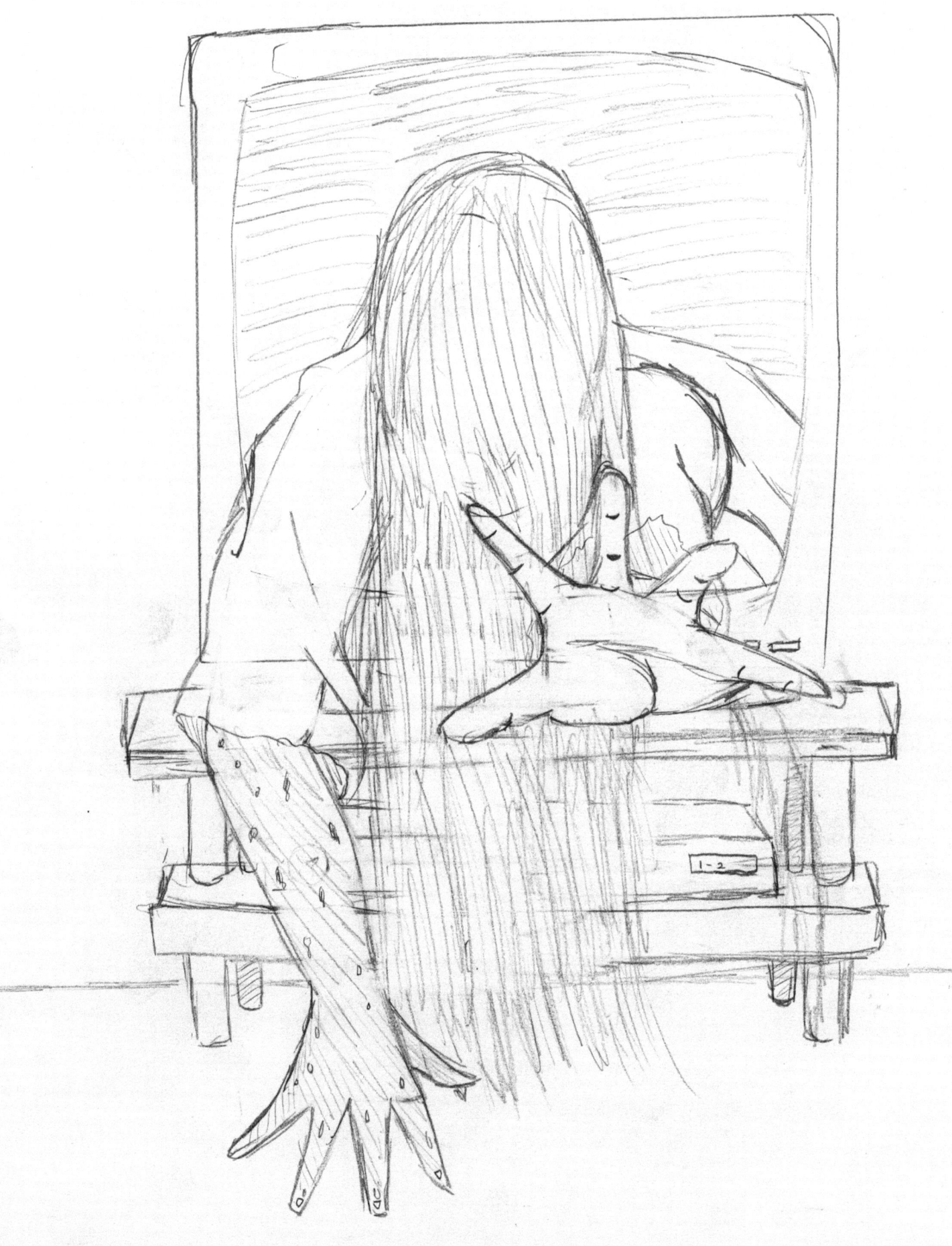

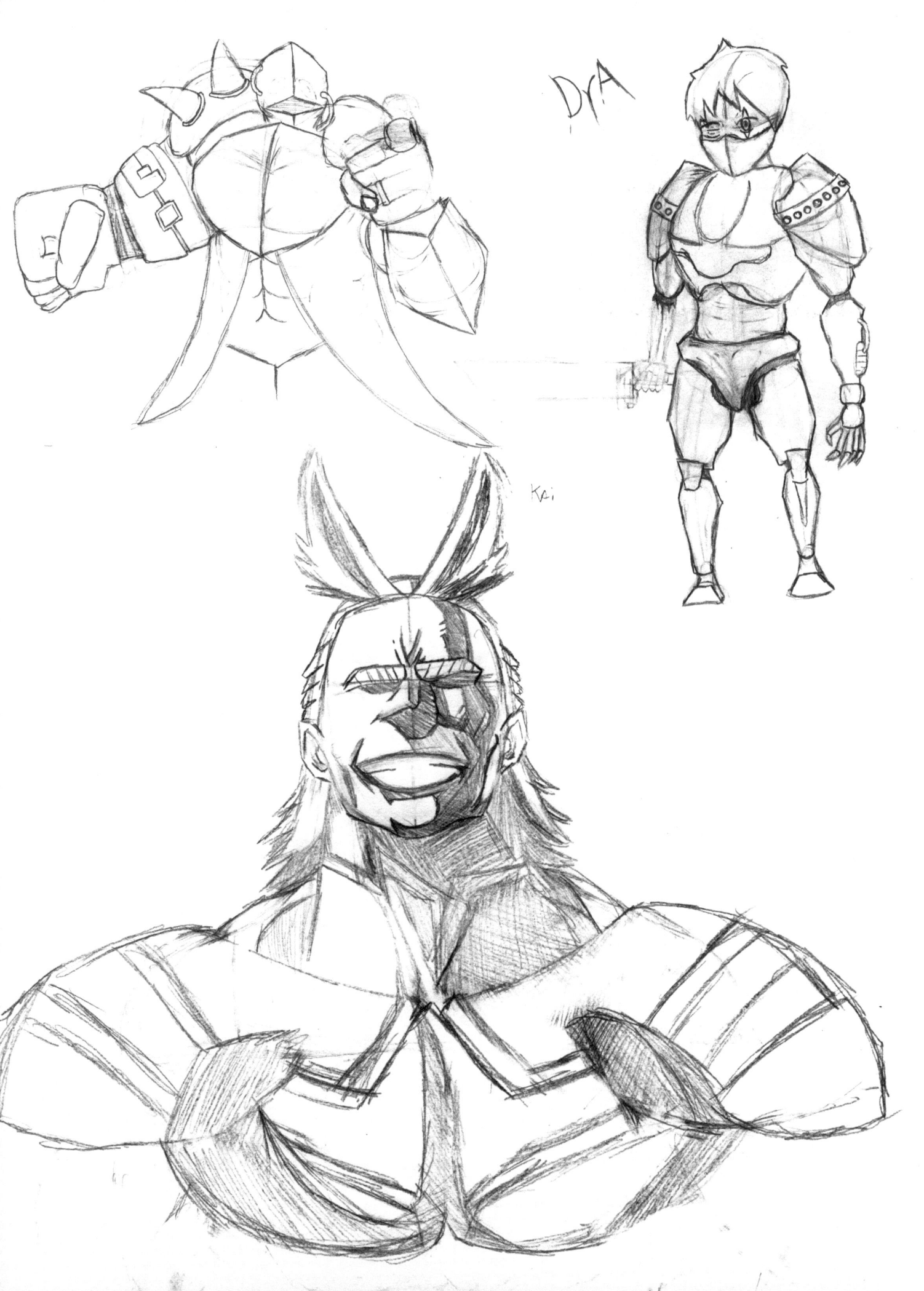

Kai

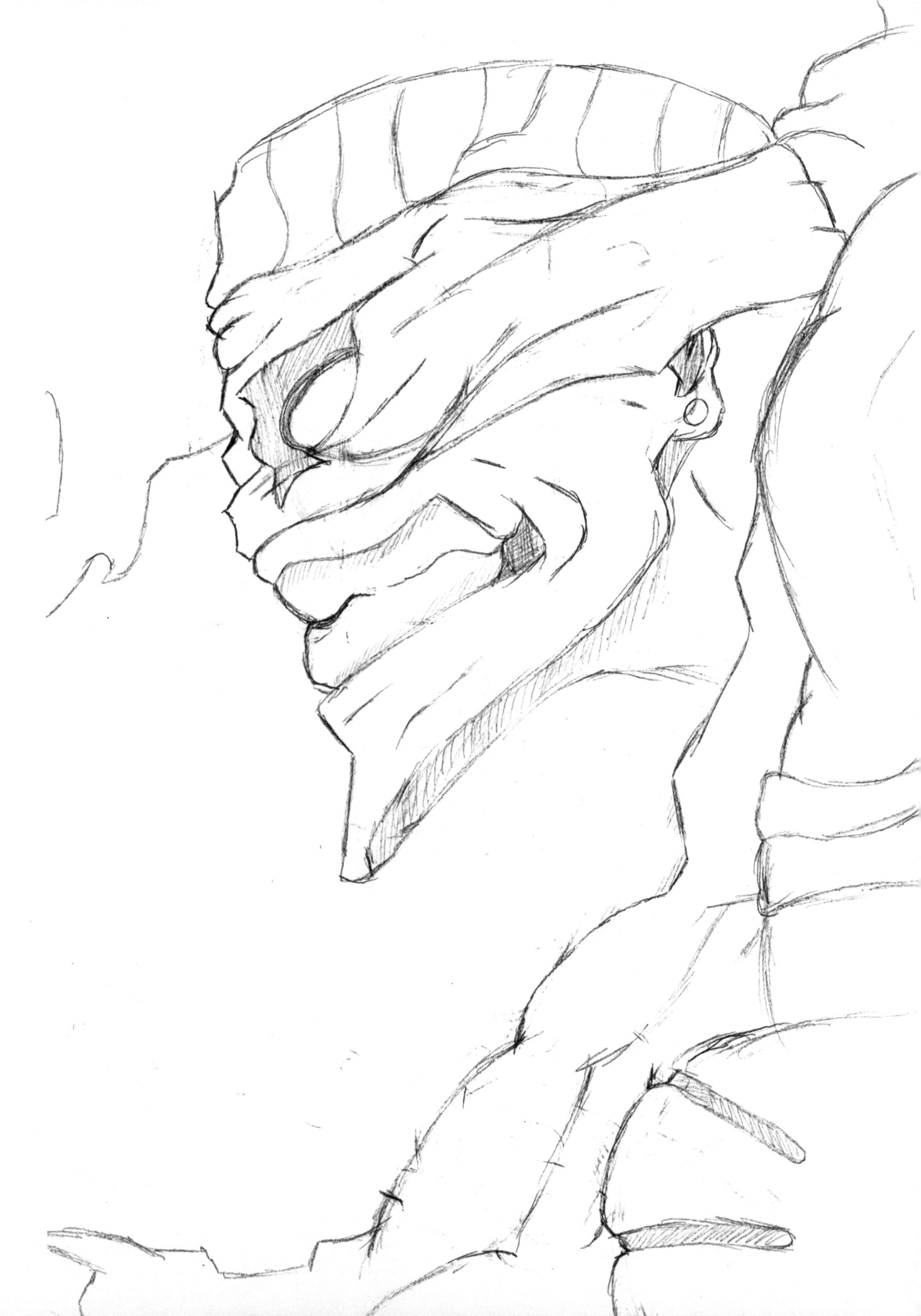

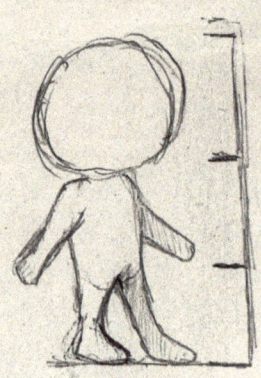
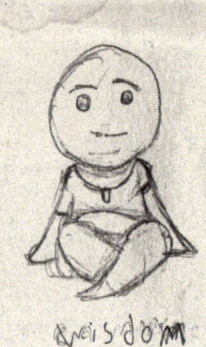
wisdom
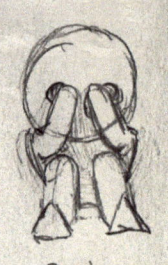
sadness

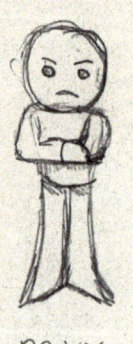
envy
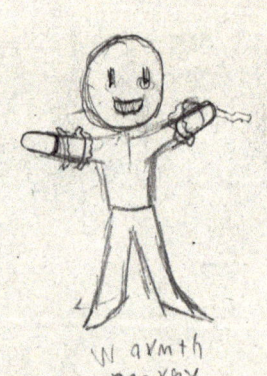
warmth
energy
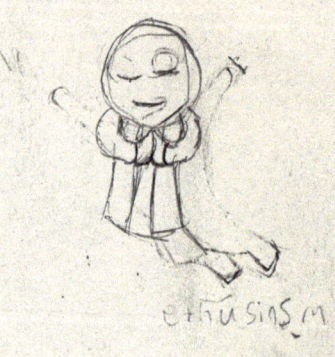
ethusinsm

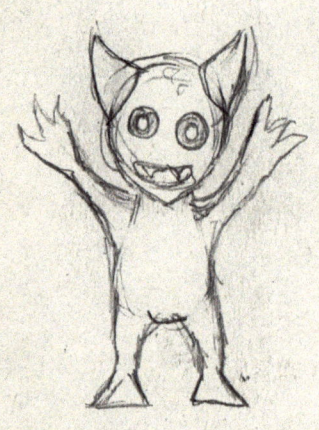
unhappiness
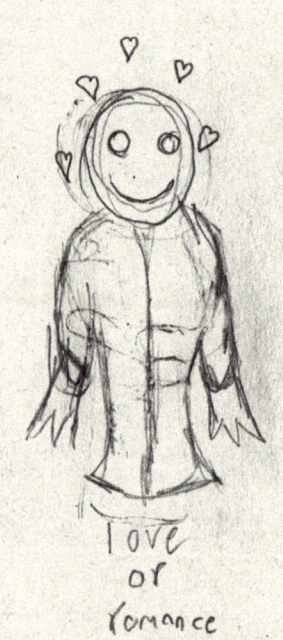
love
or
romance
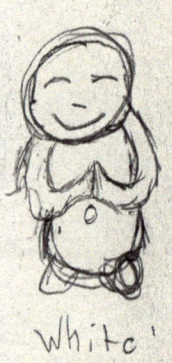
white

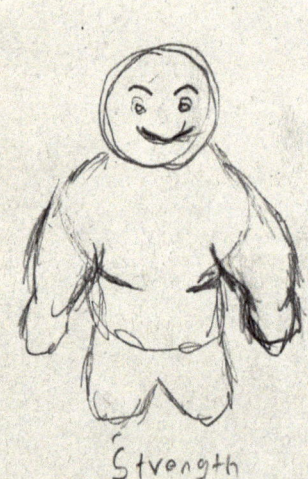
strength
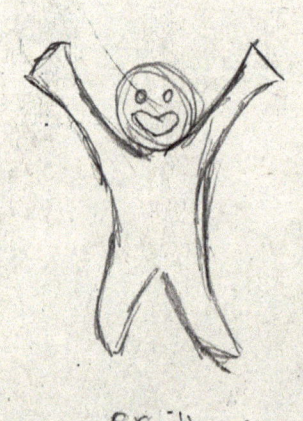
excitement
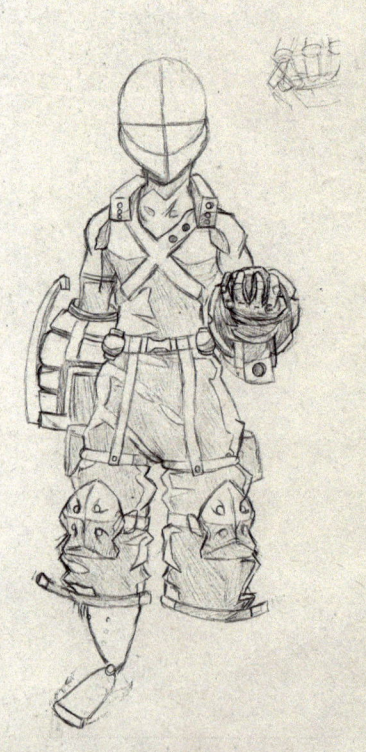

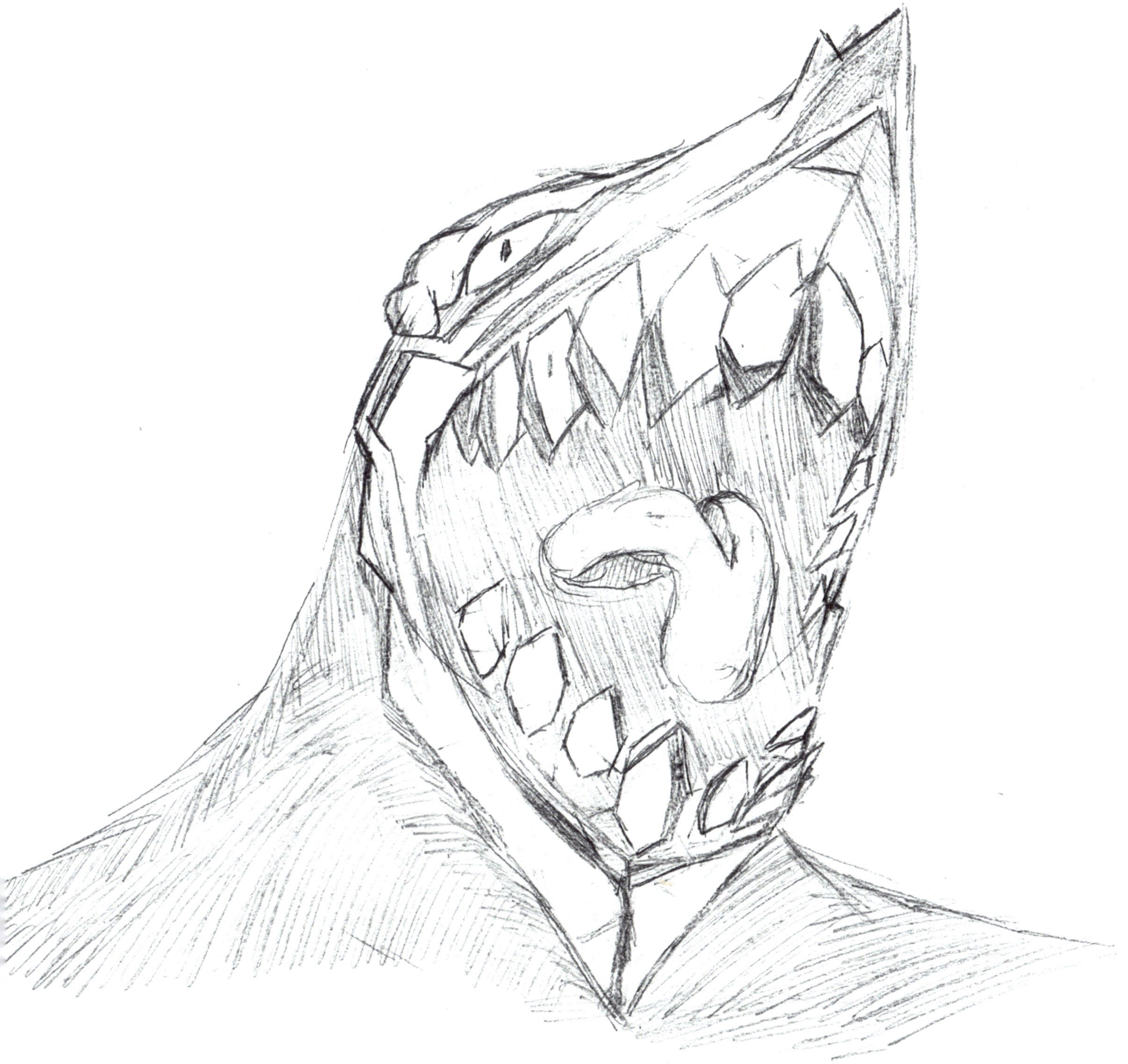

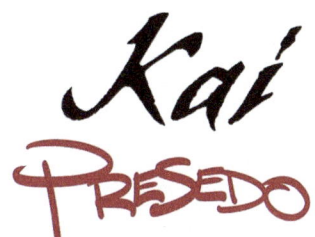

www.dramenon.com

Instagram
@theDreadArtist

Books by Daniel Presedo

Amazon.com and BarnesandNoble.com

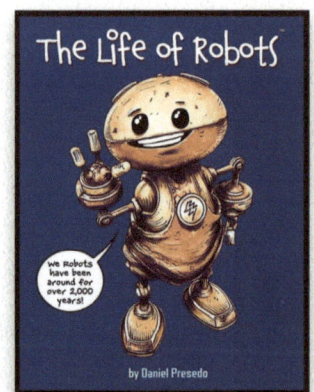
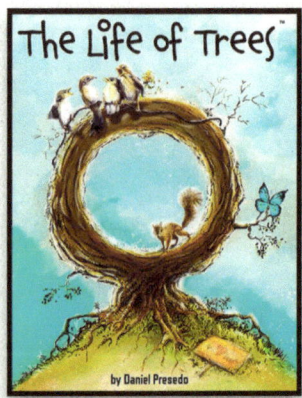
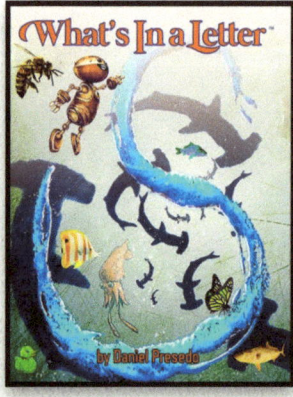
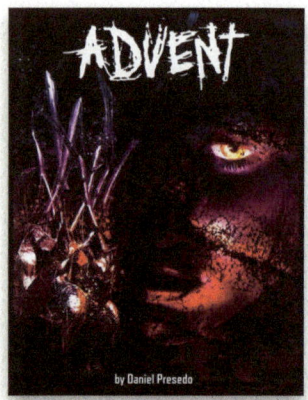
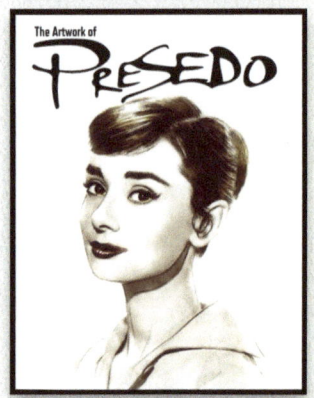
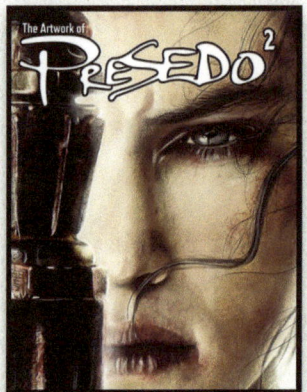
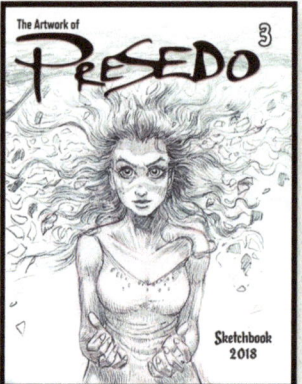
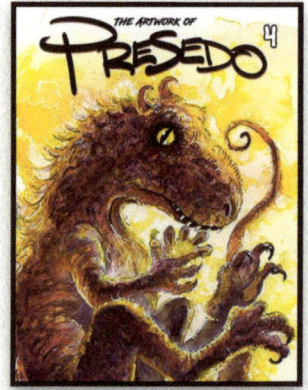
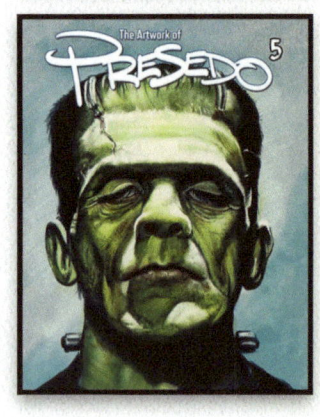
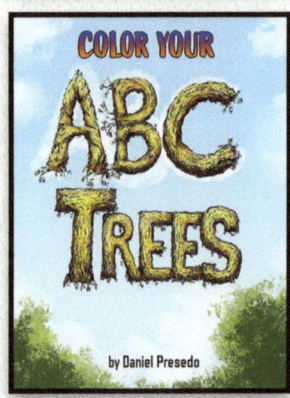
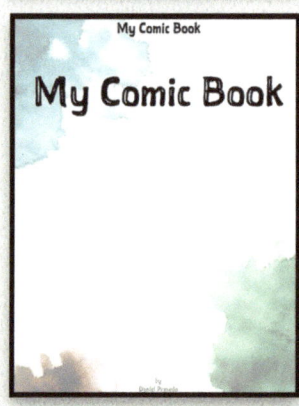
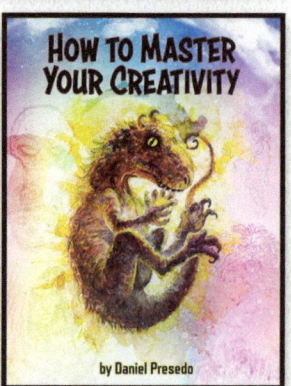

Twitter | Instagram | YouTube | Pinterest
@dramenon

www.ingramcontent.com/pod-product-compliance
Lightning Source LLC
Chambersburg PA
CBHW041935240526

45473CB00034B/1652